IT APPLICATION FOR FINANCIAL ACCOUNTING
Incorporating Sage Line 50 - Volume 1

WORKBOOK - 2017

Exploring how information technology has been integrated with financial accounting processes by modern businesses in pursuant of excellence.

Dunzo Dumzor Onwordi

AuthorHouse™ UK
1663 Liberty Drive
Bloomington, IN 47403 USA
www.authorhouse.co.uk
Phone: 0800.197.4150

Published by AuthorHouse 10/12/2017

ISBN: 978-1-5462-8144-3 (sc)
ISBN: 978-1-5462-8143-6 (e)

Foreword

By Johnnes Arreymbi

The application and use of IT in business, especially SMEs, has always posed interesting challenges. This text gives a step by step start-up guide to students who want to know about Financial Accounting and how to use the tools (as exemplified with the use of Sage in this workbook) to facilitate the process involved.

This is an excellent workbook and covers most of the areas, including hands-on exercise to develop users' confidence in Accounting and Finance in today's digital business.

Highly recommended.
Johnnes Arreymbi is a Chartered IT Professional, Chartered Fellow of the BCS and Associate Professor of Computer Sciences.

Dedication/Abstract

This book is dedicated to the Almighty God who has preserved me to this day against all obstacles and tribulations. Were it not for the fact that his words will not go void, I wouldn't have written this IT integrated financial workbook.

The main objective of this book is to assist seekers of employment in the accounting and finance industry gain hands-on experience on sage line 50. It will look into the flow process in this program through the eyes of accounting enthusiasts. Explaining the creation of account and how it is used to collate and process data for running the day to day business transactions.

Areas covered include but are not limited to buying and selling, payments and receipts, accruals and prepayments, depreciating and revaluing, borrowing and lending transactions. It will gradually explore more in subsequent volumes about how Information technology has visibly crossed path and become intertwined with the financial industry and the business world as a whole.

The drive for this book was to contribute albeit little to this industry, to thank my beautiful family for being there for me and most importantly to impress that with God first, every other thing will follow.

Thank you Lord

Dunzo Dumzor Onwordi

About this book

The business world today is at a crossroad with financial accounting and information technology. Ignoring this is at the detriment of growth and it has become a huge battle for accountants to profess solution to this. Hence having IT knowledge will give accounting professional a competitive advantage in this ever changing integrated business environment.

According to Professor Jane K Winn of the University Of Washington School Of Law, "Financial institutions were at the forefront in creating the global information economy as it exists today". Finance today relies on information technology.

In the 1960s, The New York Stock Exchange shortened it trading period to cope with the high volume of trades. The deployment of IT such as computers and other local networks improved capability and handling higher volumes became possible.

More development in this area has been encouraged by push from accountants. It has led to in information system that is versatile, robust with beneficial reduction in costs and improved speed, reliability. Amongst them are:

Equipment – such as computers, printers, scanners, faxes etc.

Software – programs, spreadsheets such as excel,

Internet – enhanced information sharing, online filing of accounts and returns etc.?

Security – confidential documents can be access only with passwords

Education – accounting and information degrees are now available in universities.

Discussion on the various elements of Information Technology will be limited here.

Volume two will explore more on the interaction of IT System with Financial Accounting as the general model of Accounting and Information System below depicted.

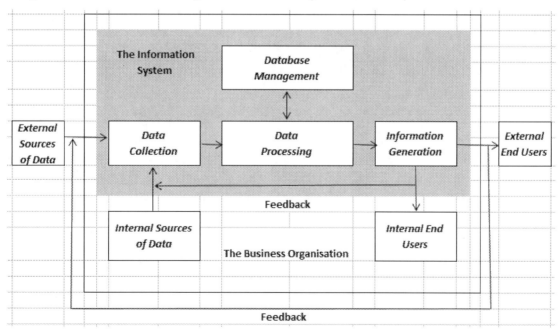

The remainder of this book will basically consider using the computer with sage line 50 as one of the IT application for Financial Accounting.

Section 1 of this book will cover the set-up of business entities on sage and how to secure a regular back-up at appropriate interval. It will look into the maintenance procedure where sage will alert users of errors and step to be taken for their correction. You will also learn to restore backed up files to the system should the need arise.

Section 2 and 3 cover the trading entities business activities involving suppliers and customers. You will learn how to set-up suppliers and customers on Sage line 50 and how to:

✓ Record suppliers invoices, apply credit notes and deal with queries

✓ Invoice customers, issue credit notes and deal with related queries.

It will also explain different modes of settlement and how they are collated for accountability.

Section 4 will look into banking. It will show how receipts from customers are applied as well as how payments to suppliers are treated on sage. It will occlude this section by explaining bank reconciliation and demonstrate these using transactions up to this book section.

Section 5 will focus on the end of month routines to produce an accurate and fair monthly management account for report to management. It will explain:

✓ Month End procedures like accrual and prepayments

✓ Financial accounting concept of accrual and prepayments and

✓ How Sage will handle simple accrual and prepayment situation by journal.

Section6 will explain the financial accounting treatment of fixed assets (i.e. Non-Current Assets) and depreciation. It will demonstrate two methods of fixed assets depreciation methods. It briefly explains simple sage treatment of fixed assets and depreciation without activating depreciation auto run. This is outside the scope of this book

As you go through each Section, quick comprehensive exercises and tests will be attempted and answered to consolidate both academic and practical knowledge of financial accounting using Sage line 50 for practical record keeping experience.

Section 7 will end the volume by going through a comprehensive exercise on adjustment of Trial Balance (i.e. the extracted general ledger balances). From this, a comprehensive income statement (profit and loss account) and statement of financial position (the balance sheet) will be produced.

Table of Contents

BLANK PAGE

Note

Section 1.0: Section Coverage Overview

Before the advent of computers, accounting records were kept manually. They were written down on books in form termed T- Accounts. Accounting activities were recorded in ledgers with links between them that explain their sources and destinations. This is the double entry bookkeeping principle that ensures every debit have corresponding credit and vice versa.

Businesses are now been maintained in paperless forms in computers - Accounts are now coded in machine readable codes. These are the nominal codes. It will not make sense if these codes are left loose without proper order. By order means proper grouping of these codes in analytical and reportable forms. This gave birth to charting account in codes hence the name, the Chart of Account (COA). An improvement to the COA is the

creation of departments to further enhance control and scrutiny of certain elements of accounting operation.

Section 1.1: Creating New Account on Sage

In this first Section, you will learn:

- ✓ How to create business account on sage
- ✓ How to format the Chart of Account
- ✓ How to format Departmental code

The company that will be used to run this course is OSPAC LTD. By creating this company and formatting all the structure, it will be possible to collate data and produce the reports that will be useful to users of financial statements. This user groups include but are not limited to:

User Group	Needs information for
Management	Control of costs, improved profitability
Lenders	Borrowing and credit purposes
Shareholders and investment analysts	Investment decisions – buying and selling shares
Governments	Need to be able to assess taxation and regulate industries, as well as using information for statistical purposes
Employees	Trade unions and so on need information to be able to employer's stability and profitability, and their ability to provide remuneration and other benefits
Customers	Will want to judge whether the company will continue in existence, especially where they have a long term involvement with the company or dependence on its products

BLANK PAGE

Creating Account on Sage Line 50

Once you log on to Sage Line 50, you will be prompted to the screen below:

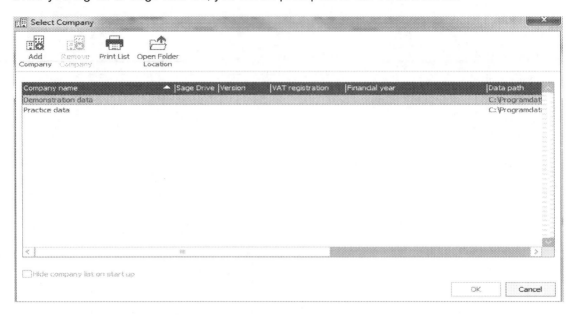

As you are creating a brand new business, you will avoid those on the list under **company name** and select the ***Add Company*** option above.

Click on ***Add Company*** and the screen below pops up:

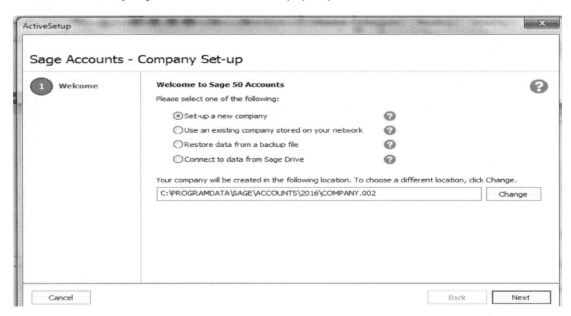

This is the **Wizard.**

As you move through the wizard, it prompts you to enter details about your company, such as company name, address, phone numbers, and the type of business and industry in which you work.

BLANK PAGE

Note

Click the **Next button** to move forward, or the **Back button** to go back and review the information you entered. If you get stuck, click the **Help** button for assistance.

- Enter your company name and address information.

- Enter your **fiscal year Start** and **End dates.**

Let Sage 50 Line create the list of accounts that you will use to track your business.

Some accounts are industry-specific, so select your industry to get the list of accounts that best suits your business needs. If you do not know which type to pick, select **other**.

- You can always modify your account list later.

- If you're just starting out, let Sage 50 create a list of accounts for you.

- Select your ownership structure, industry type.

- **Click View List of Accounts** to view the complete list of accounts that will be created for your company.

- Accept the suggested file name (your company name), or enter a different name.

- Accept the suggested location or Browse to navigate to a different folder.

- Click **Finish** and Sage 50 Line will create your company.

- Follow steps, to change the date displayed on the <Standard> Balance Sheet.

- September 30 ending balances is October 1, yyyy beginning balances. Display the balance sheet for September 30 so you can check that you entered chart of accounts beginning balances correctly.

BLANK PAGE

Note

Section 1.2: Formatting the Chart of Account

Sage line 50 is created with diversified structure for difference types of business. It enhances compliance with IAS 1 – Presentation of Financial Statements (Picker, Leo, & Alfredson, 2013), such that accounts are charted in a way to produced comprehensive account for reporting compliance. This structure is termed the Chart of Account (COA). Codes of accounts have to fall within the proper range to be able to appear at the appropriate section of the financial statements. This mirrors the typical format of Income statement and balance sheet. Before you proceed, answer the following test-yourself quick questions:

Definition: A Chart of account can be stated to be a division of business financial activities into capital and revenue with a further breakdown of these two sections to function types for better reporting and analysis. All these small parts are called nominal ledger accounts for proper analysis of income, expenditure, assets,

Question

1.01   What is the chart of accounts?

1.02   List four assets accounts, two liability accounts, two equity accounts, one revenue account and three expense accounts

1.03   What is the trial balance?

NOTE

Answer on page 13.

Refer to a trial balance on page 17.

BLANK PAGE: *for study notes*		
Ans (a)		
A Chart of account can be stated to be a division of business financial activities into capital and revenue with		
a further breakdown of this two sections to function types for better reporting and analysis. All these parts		
are then coded in either alpha, numeric or alpha numeric standard names for ease of reference.		
This small parts are called nominal ledger accounts for proper analysis of income, expenditure, assets,		
Liabilities and capital of any going busines concern.		
Ans (b) 1	CA	NCA
4 assets amongst others are:		
Building		NCA
Plant		NCA
Inventory	CA	
Debtor/Receivable	CA	
Ans (b) 2	CL	NCL
2 Liabilities amongst others are:		
Debentures		NCL
Creditor/Payable	CL	
Ans (b) 3	EQ	
2 Equity Accounts amongst others are:		
Share capital	EQ	
Share premium	EQ	
Ans (b) 4	Rev	
1 Revenue account amongst others are:		
Retained profit (as this arise from excess profit from trading activities)	Rev	
Ans (b) 5	Dist	Adm
3 Expense account amongst others are:		
Salesmen	Dist	
Delivery van expenses	Dist	
Office rent and retae		Adm
Ans (c)		
What is the trial balance?		
Trial balance is the list of all the T-accounts from the geneeral ledger of a business.		
This are the balances of all the doble entries that has passed through during the normal business		
transactions. In book keeping, every debit mist have a corresponding credit, As such the extaration of all		
the t-accounts MUST balance; hence the name Trial BALANCE.		
Please note that:		
NCA= Non current asset		
CA= Current asset		
NCL= Non current liabilities		
EQ= Equity		
Rev= Revenue		
Dist= Distribution		
Adm= Administration		
Note		

Section 1.3: Formatting the Departmental code

What is departmental code?

Definition: *Department represent section of an operation to enable specific scrutiny of income and expenses. These departments are named in form of codes so that analysis can be drawn for relevant data attributable to these departments, hence departmental codes.*

Departmental code is prevalent when various sections have freedom of control over income and expenses. By allocating department code to departments, sections can be examined individually.

Creating departmental code.

From Sage Line 50 panel:

   ✓ Select Department

The pre-numbered list of departments up 999 with 0 as default appears as shown below:

Double click on the number you what to allocate to a department and the window below appears:

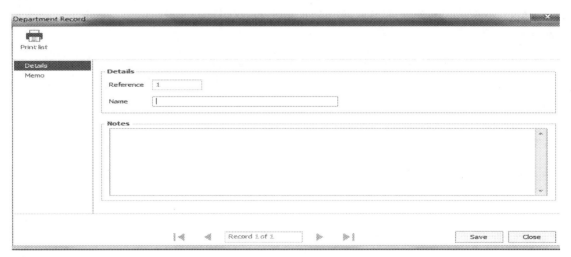

Name the department and Click the SAVE button to save and exit.

BLANK PAGE

Note

Section 1.4: Primary entries to the created account

Before you move on to the rest of the sections it will be proper, as this business is a limited company, to pass some of the main entries that gave it the status of a legal entity. There will be two journal entries here. This first will take care of the company's formation costs while the second will take care of the issue of shares to the first shareholders of the limited company. The first shareholder of OSPAC Ltd is the director; D. D. Onward (DDO).

Above is relevant to limited liability companies. Other mode of operation such as sole trader, Charities, will have set up costs peculiar to their own nature.

For OSPAC Ltd, it cost the director, DDO, 150on 01/01/yyyy to form the company and 5,000 to acquire 10,000 unit of ordinary share of .50 each on the same date.

Question

1.04   Pass the necessary journal entries to take record above transactions.

Journal 1:
Debit formation cost   150
              Credit Directors current account   150

Being formation cost for OSPAC Ltd paid by DDO

Journal 2:
Debit Cash and Bank Account   5,000
        Credit   Ordinary Share capital account   5,000

Being issue of 10,000 ordinary share of 0.50 share each to DDO.

T - ACCOUNTS				TRIAL BALANCE	(TB)	
				T - Accounts extracted	DR	CR
F1/01 - Formation costs	DR	CR				
Narration						
01/01/yyyy:D.D. Onwordi						
Formation costs	150.00					
xxx						
B/cfwd	-	150.00				
B/bfwd	150.00	-		F1/01 - Formation costs	150.00	-
F2/01 - Director Current Account - D. D. Onward	DR	CR				
Narration						
01/01/yyyy:D.D. Onwordi						
Formation costs		150.00				
xxx						
B/cfwd	150.00	-				
B/bfwd	-	150.00		F2/01 - Director Current Account - D. D	-	150.00
9/01 - Bank Current A/c -1200	DR	CR				
Narration						
01/01/yyyy:10,000 share of .50	5,000.00					
xxx						
B/cfwd	-	5,000.00				
B/bfwd	5,000.00	-		9/01 - Bank Current A/c -1200	5,000.00	-
0/02 - Share apital	DR	CR				
Narration						
01/01/yyyy:10,000 share of .50 fully paid		5,000.00				
xxx						
B/cfwd	5,000.00	-				
B/bfwd	-	5,000.00		0/02 - Share apital	-	5,000.00
Office use only				**Grand Total of all accounts**		
Form Forma1				*balances to date:>>*	5,150.00	5,150.00

Section 2.0: Section Coverage Overview

> To continue trading, businesses will maintain their stock at an appropriate level. These products are made available by others called suppliers. As businesses need to buy some of these products on credit so these suppliers will be carried as payables (i.e. creditors) in the books.
>
> You will learn how to create these suppliers on Sage line 50, run the basic activities and record settlement of indebtedness on sage. You will also learn how to communicate financial activities and balances for prompt settlements and the steps to take to bring serious outstanding balances to each other's attention.

Section 2.1: Suppliers

Definition: *These are business associates from whom goods and/or services are bought from either in cash or credit. When items are purchased on credit, these associates will be carried in the buyers' books as creditors / payables until these indebtedness's are fully settled in cash or kind.*

OSPAC LTD will be the business that will be use for illustration in this book and you will be working for it. It will carry these suppliers in its books when it buys things ON CREDIT.

To obtain credit facility from a supplier, some credit references might be checked such as:

- ✓ Bank reference – to ascertain if the customer can pay for the goods/services
- ✓ Trade reference – to ascertain from other businesses dealt with if terms are observed
    - o Example of credit payment terms are net 30 days (Payment 30 days after invoice date)

Section 2.2: Dealing with Suppliers and related transactions

In this Section, you will learn to:

- ✓ Navigate the sage Suppliers Section
- ✓ Familiarize yourself with the flow of processes and terminologies, then you will:
    - o SET-UP SUPPLIERS IN SAGE
    - o ENTER/POST: Invoices, Credit notes, using batch processing & Flag items as items on dispute.

    (The other option is to post via the purchase order update route. This and product set-up are outside this volume)

Example A – Purchase Transaction

OSPAC LTD purchased 3 computers from COMPUTER LAND LTD. The details below are relevant:

Date of purchase –a (06/01/yyyy)

Invoice reference - com0001

Price including vat - 550.00 each

BLANK PAGE

Note

1st Requirement: Set-up the Supplier using the wizard option

Set-up COMPUTER LAND LTD in sage using their details given below:

Supplier's name -COMPUTER LAND LTD

A/c code - COMP01 (In this book, it is recommended to use the first 4 letter of the Associates' names followed by 01….n)

Address
Unit 2 Computer Land
Romford RM3 3DD
Select Tax code - T1 from the drop down list
Vat registration no   - 66 6999 911
Select Nominal code - 0030 from Drop down list
*Tick -**Term agreed** in Credit control section*

Action

*Select **Suppliers** from the list displayed on the left hand panel:*

The screen below will pop-up

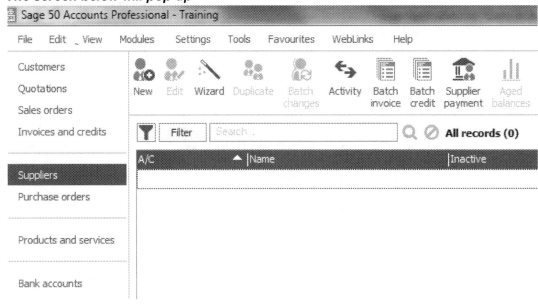

BLANK PAGE

Note

23

*Click the **NEW** icon on the screen above. The screen below appears.*

Now begin to input all the given information methodically starting from
- ✓ *Details*
- ✓ *Defaults*
- ✓ *Credit Control .and so on as necessary (skipping cells not necessary or compulsory).*

2ⁿᵈ Requirement: Enter/Post the Invoice

Post the invoice from Computer Land Ltd via Batch Invoice and answer the question below. Here are the details again:

OSPAC LTD purchased:
- *3 computers from COMPUTER LAND LTD*
- *Date of purchase - 06/01/YYYY*
- *Invoice reference - com0001*
- *Price including vat - 550.00*

Action
*Goto **Suppliers***

➢ *Click **Batch invoice** on the screen, and the next window will appear*

BLANK PAGE

Note

Here is the screen below:

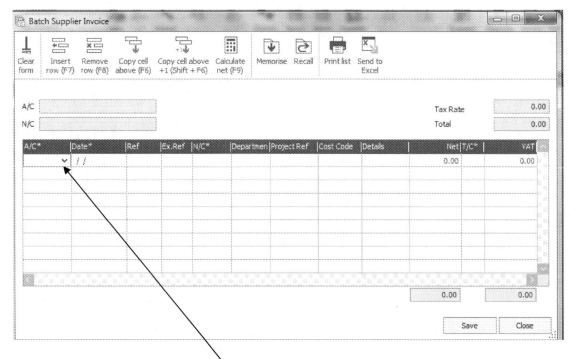

Now activate the Drop Down list @ **AC***

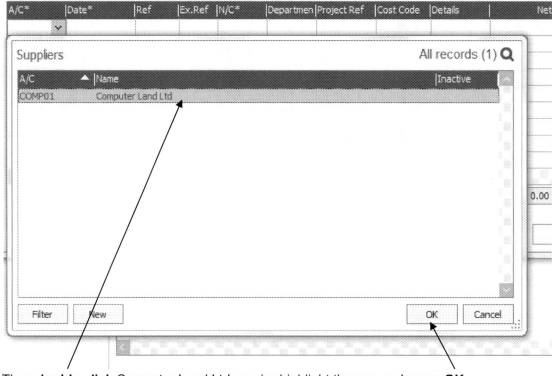

Then **double click** Computer Land Ltd row (or highlight the row and press **OK** button)

BLANK PAGE

The batch invoice window below will appear. **Computer Land Ltd** will appear in A/C box as it's currently been processed. Once you leave the row the next supplier to be posted will occupy this box.

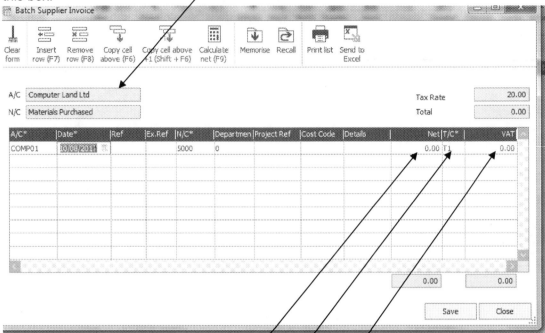

✓ Enter all the information on the above on the screen but NOTE!!
  o Including vat means that the **550.00** is gross.
  o You need to derive the net figure by *dividing **550.00** by 1.2 (as vat rate is 20%) = **458.33** (use the calculator in the amount box)*
✓ *Post the total i.e. **458.33** x 3 = **1375.00**…………… in the **Net** BOX*

The vat amount will automatically appear as **275.00** in the VAT BOX as the default tax code is 20%) If at this point or any other time, the vat rate is not T1, you can change the tax code for the transaction from the **T/C*** Box to the appropriate tax code)

A total amount/gross of **1,650.00** will be noticed in the **Total** box as this is the first entry in the batch screen. This box is a cumulative box as subsequent gross figures will be added to this.)

✓ Click **Save** to finish posting

BLANK PAGE

Question

On this Particular transaction

2.01   How much do you owe *COMPUTER LAND LTD?* **1,650.00**

2.02   How much will appear in the Profit and loss account? **None**

2.03   How much of this transaction will be posted to VAT A/C? **275.00**

2.04   Is the vat a debit or credit amount? **Debit**

2.05   Where will the computers appear in the financial statement? Income statement or
balance sheet and what value will be attributed to them? **balance sheet at 1,375.00**

T - Accounts continue from page 19

T - ACCOUNTS				TRIAL BALANCE		{ TB }	
				T - Accounts extracted		DR	CR
1/01 - Computers	DR	CR					
Narration							
06/01/yyyy: COMP01,,,,,,3 Laptops @ 550 ea	1,375.00						
xxx							
B/cfwd	-	1,375.00					
B/bfwd	1,375.00	-		1/01 - Computers		1,375.00	-
2/01 - VAT Control a/c	DR	CR					
Narration							
06/01/yyyy: COMP01,,,VAT, 3 Laptops @ 550 ea	275.00						
xxx							
B/cfwd	-	275.00					
B/bfwd	275.00	-		2/01 - VAT Control a/c		275.00	-
3/01 - COMP01: Computer Land Ltd	DR	CR					
Narration							
06/01/yyyy: Computers:,,, 3 Laptops @ 550 ea		1,650.00					
xxx							
B/cfwd	1,650.00	-					
B/bfwd	-	1,650.00		3/01 - COMP01: Computer Land Ltd		-	1,650.00
				Balances of accounts			
				not currently actioned here:			
-					-	-	-
					-	-	-
				F1/01 - Formation costs		150.00	-
				F2/01 - Director Current Account - D. D. Onward		-	150.00
				9/01 - Bank Current A/c -1200		5,000.00	-
				0/02 - Share apital		-	5,000.00
Office use only				*Grand Total of all accounts*			
Form A				*balances to date:>>*		6,800.00	6,800.00

Example B – Purchase Transaction

OSPAC Ltd bought stationary from OFFICE STATIONERS LTD on credit for office use and the relevant information are given below:

> OFFICE STATIONERS LTD
>
> 7 Mount Pleasant
>
> London
>
> WC1 7PP
>
> Vat Reg: GB 67 6929 291
>
> *Date of purchase –08/02/YYYY*
>
> *Invoice reference - off101*
>
> *Price excluding vat - 200.00*

Required

Set-up OFFICE STATIONERS LTD in sage via Batch Invoice processing:

Action

Goto **Suppliers**
- ✓ **Batch Invoice**
- ✓ Enter the account code using the company's (i.e. OSPAC LTD's) established standard coding method; and since this is the first time dealing with this supplier and not previously created, you will be prompted to create it.
- ✓ Proceed normally (as previously discussed) and create the NEW supplier.
- ✓ Enter all the relevant information.
  - E.g. default nominal account code for this type of transaction if constant other skip
  - Vat rate type from this transaction if applicable
  - Credit terms agreed, otherwise
    - Click Term agreed (If you don't, you will always be alerted that terms has not been agreed; this can be very irritating!)
    - Click the **default** Tab, then
      - Under Miscellaneous Default section, **select Nominal Code 7504**assuming you only purchase stationary from this supplier. **Note:** you can always change the nominal code during posting as appropriate.
    - Click **Save** and then select **OK** to continue inputting transactions.

Now Post the transaction from above data and answer the questions below:

BLANK PAGE

Note

Question

2.06   How much do you owe Office Stationers? **240**
2.07   How much do you owe all our Suppliers so far? ***1,650.00 + 240.00 = 1,890.00 ****
2.08   How much is the vat on the P&L a/c? ***None***
2.09   How much will appear in the P&L a/c? ***200***
2.10   How much will be the balance on the A/C including that from Q1.03 ***315.00***
2.11   Is this vat payable to HMC&E or reclaimable from them? Reclaimable

*

List of Suppliers Balances						
A/c Code	Suppliers Names	Account Balance				
COMP01	COMPUTER LAND LTD	1,650.00				
OFFI01	OFFICE SUPPLIERS LTD	240.00				
		1,890.00				

Invoices in dispute:

 Via Supplier > Dispute > select supplier >highlight disputed item > click dispute tab.

You now found that an invoice for printing materials from office stationers include items not ordered.

Exercise 1

Flag this invoice as invoice in dispute to prevent accidental payment until the error is rectified.

Note: If you attempt to pay an invoice that is in dispute, a warning massage will appear. You can continue to pay the invoice but if you choose to do this the dispute flag is automatically removed.
Note: you must first create dispute reasons from the configuration under settings
Extracting list of suppliers balance summary for items due for payment

T- Accounts continues from page 31

T - ACCOUNTS			TRIAL BALANCE		(TB)
			T - Accounts extracted	DR	CR
4/01 - Stationary	DR	CR			
Narration					
08/02/yyyy: OFFI01,,Stationary @200 ex vat	200.00				
xxx					
B/cfwd	-	200.00			
	200.00	200.00			
B/bfwd	200.00	-	4/01 - Stationary	200.00	-
2/02 - VAT Control a/c	DR	CR			
Narration					
06/01/yyyy: COMP01,,VAT, 3 Laptops @ 550 ea	275.00				
08/01/yyyy: OFFI01,,Vat on Stationary	40.00				
xxx					
B/cfwd	-	315.00			
	315.00	315.00			
B/bfwd	315.00	-	2/02 - VAT Control a/c	315.00	-
5/01 - OFFI01: Office Stationers Ltd	DR	CR			
Narration					
08/02/yyyy:,,Stationary @ 200 ex-vat		240.00			
xxx					
B/cfwd	240.00	-			
	240.00	240.00			
B/bfwd	-	240.00	5/01 - OFFI01: Office Stationers Ltd	-	240.00
			Balances of accounts		
Previous accounts actioned to date			*not currently actioned here:*		
			F1/01 - Formation costs	150.00	-
			F2/01 - Director Current Account - D. D	-	150.00
			9/01 - Bank Current A/c -1200	5,000.00	-
			0/02 - Share apital	-	5,000.00
			1/01 - Computers	1,375.00	-
			3/01 - COMP01: Computer Land Ltd	-	1,650.00
Office use only			*Grand Total of all accounts*		
Form B			*balances to date:>>*	7,040.00	7,040.00

Extracting suppliers Invoices Due

Goto report in the link list

Goto **Supplier Invoices** reports – Expand the list by double clicking on the + sign

Double click on **Suppliers Invoices due**. Below window will appear

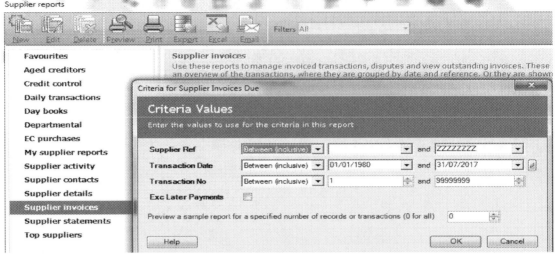

Enter the **Transaction dates"** for which you want to make payment in the "**From**" "**to**" cells

to select all Suppliers balances.

Click "**OK**". List of Suppliers balances due will then appear as below:

Date:	31/07/2017		OSPAC LTD			Page:	1
Time:	18:25:32		**Supplier Invoices Due**				

Supplier From:				Date From:	01/01/1980
Supplier To:	ZZZZZZZZ			Date To:	31/07/2017
Transaction From:	1			Exc Later Payments:	No
Transaction To:	99,999,999				

A/C:	COMP01	**Name:**	COMPUTER LAND LTD	Contact:		Tel:	

No	Type	Ref	Date	Details		Amount	Paid	Outstanding
1	PI		27/06/2017	Apple		1,650.00	0.00	1,650.00
					Total:			1,650.00

A/C:	OFFI01	**Name:**	OFFICE STATIONERS LTD	Contact:	John	Tel:	

No	Type	Ref	Date	Details		Amount	Paid	Outstanding
2	PI	of4001	07/06/2017	Stationary		240.00	0.00	240.00
					Total:			240.00
					Grand Total			1,890.00

Check items on the list to physical invoices before writing cheques to suppliers.

Note (From reconciliation of suppliers statement)

Above procedures could be used to reconcile suppliers' statement for accuracy so long as

transaction dates on statements from both Parties are matched

BLANK PAGE

Note

Section 2.3: Batch Invoicing (Suppliers)

In Section 2.2 Example B, you set up Office Stationary Ltd in sage by an attempt to post the invoice through batch invoicing. This is to learn set up via this route. The purpose of this part is to post more than one invoice from one or more suppliers from one batch screen.

Below are vital extracts from various invoices received from suppliers:

Customers Name	Account Code	Invoice date	Invoice Ref	Order Ref	Good/Serv ices	Pro Type	Nom Code	Qt y	Net Amount	Vat	Gross Amount	Postal Address
Plastic Binders Ltd	PLAS01	20/01/2017	PL0001	DDO	Binders	Product	4000	100	250	50	300	N/a
Rent to Kill Ltd	RENT01	20/01/2017	Inv8705	DDO	Detergents	Product	4000	15	89.85	18	107.82	N/a

You are required to enter these invoices in the central sage system

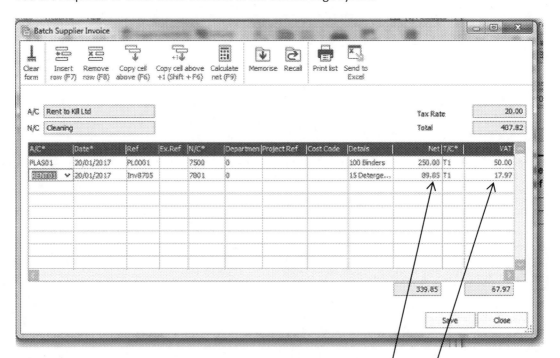

At the end of the whole batch, click **SAVE** and the entries will disappear as now posted to the various suppliers' account and debited to the respective nominal ledger.

The double entries for each row in the batch screen can be explained using Rent To Kill (the last entry) for explanation:

Cleaning is **7801** debited with   89.85
VAT (**Purchase vat control account**) is debited with: 17.97

  (Because you are in business, you will get the vat refunded hence a debit to Custom & Excise)

Rent To Kill is credited with the net income: (the net 89.85 + vat 17.97)   107.82

Please note, above entries will not appear in the T - accounts. They are for demonstration only.

BLANK PAGE

Note

Section 3.0: Section Coverage Overview

Customers are the life line of any profit oriented establishment. This is why businesses will take actions such as intense advertising or lower prices to attract large customer base. In this section, you will learn how to set customer up on sage and maintain them, take orders and invoice them, record payment from them and communicate outstanding balances to them at appropriate level of severity.

Section 3.1: Customers

Definition: *These are business associates to whom goods and/or services are sold to either in cash or credit. When items are sold on credit, they will be carried as debtors / receivable in the sellers' books until these indebtedness's are fully settled in cash or kind.*

Here you are dealing with sales to customers on credit. They will be carried in your book as debtors until you receive payments for all the goods/services sold/rendered to them.

Section 3.2: Dealing with Customers and related transactions

Invoicing

This can be either

- ✓ Invoicing via Configured Products

- ✓ Invoicing via Special Products

- ✓ Invoicing for non-credit sales

Section 3.3: Invoicing via Configured Products

Product configuration is outside the scope of this volume. However it is worthy of note that it enhances the process of invoicing from pre-set product lines such that details can be automatically posted to customers invoices.

In this volume, invoices will be produced using the special product lines as will be discussed in next Section 3.4.

BLANK PAGE

Note

Section 3.4: Invoicing via Special Products

You will not configure products in this volume as stated in Section 3.3. This is outside this volume. As you procure product for resale, you will apply traditional methods and keep a manual record of stock in and stock out. From this record, you will derive your closing stock position for final adjustments to your cost of sales. Since you are going to learn invoicing in this section, you will quickly record the purchases from Best Producers Ltd for books you are about to sell to your next two customers. However, invoices can be raised by using the special products or services line provided by sage.

Below are the details the purchase of books from Best Producers Ltd:

Name: BEST PRODUCERS LTD
Address: 21 London Road
                Romford, RM2 6BT
Vat reg: GB 826996295
Nominal code: **5000**
Tax Code: **T0**

Bought 1,000 books on *"Introduction to OSPAC Financial Accounting Systems"* at 15 each

Set up the supplier for this purchase of Books:
(Follow the discussion from earlier sections)

Example C (i)

You sold 10 books to UNIVERSAL LIBRARY LTD. See details below:

Sold: 10 books
Date: 09/02/yyyy
Our Ref: 10703
Total sales value   200 vat exempt
Use code   **UNIV01**
Item sold   Introduction to OSPAC Financial Accounting Systems

Create the invoice for the sales **via *Special Invoicing*** using relevant details above.

Select one of the **special products or services** and proceed to complete the invoice for Universal Library Ltd. (Go to **Example C (ii) Exercise2.** on page 48 for the relevant steps)

Questions
3.01   How much do UNIVERSAL LIBRARY LTD owe us?***200.00***

3.02   How much revenue have you generated so far from the sale of Books**200.00**

3.03   How much will be posted to the VAT account from the sales of 10 books? **0.00**

3.04   Is it a debit or credit figure? **Not applicable**
To ensure accurate balance of debtors, all non-batch processed invoices have to be posted.

T- Accounts continue from page 35

T - ACCOUNTS	DR	CR
6/01 - BEST01: BEST PRODUCERS LTD	DR	CR
Narration		
09/02/YYYY:1,000 Books @ 15		15,000.00
xxx		
B/cfwd	15,000.00	-
B/bfwd	-	15,000.00
7/01 - Purchases	DR	CR
Narration		
09/02/YYYY:BEST01,,1,000 Books @ 15	15,000.00	
xxx		
B/cfwd	-	15,000.00
B/bfwd	15,000.00	-
8/01 –UNIV01: UNIVERSAL LIBRARY LTD	DR	CR
Narration		
09/02/YYYY: ,,Sales 10 books @20 ea	200.00	
xxx		
B/cfwd	-	200.00
B/bfwd	200.00	-
9/01 -Books Sales	DR	CR
Narration		
09/02/YYYY: UNIV01,,Sales 10 books @20 ea		200.00
xxx		
B/cfwd	200.00	-
B/bfwd	-	200.00

TRIAL BALANCE		(TB)	
T - Accounts extracted		DR	CR
6/01 - BEST01: BEST PRODUCERS LTD		-	15,000.00
7/01 - Purchases		15,000.00	-
8/01 -UNIV01: UNIVERSAL LIBRARY LTD		200.00	-
9/01 -Books Sales		-	200.00
Balances of accounts			
not currently actioned here:			
	-	-	-
F1/01 - Formation costs		150.00	-
F2/01 - Director Current Account - D. D. Or		-	150.00
9/01 - Bank Current A/c -1200		5,000.00	-
0/02 - Share apital		-	5,000.00
1/01 - Computers		1,375.00	-
3/01 - COMP01: Computer Land Ltd		-	1,650.00
5/01 - OFFI01: Office Stationers Ltd		-	240.00
4/01 - Stationary		200.00	-
2/02 - VAT Control a/c		315.00	-

Office use only		
Form C		

	Grand Total of all accounts		
	balances to date:>>	22,240.00	22,240.00

Example C (ii)

You sold another batch 400 of these books to **STAR LIBRIRY EDUCTIONIST LTD** at 20 each. This is your first transaction with them. From the manual invoice produced by OSPAC LTD, the following can be sighted:

✓ Business address: 11 Smart land
Dagenham
RM10 7PP

✓ VAT Reg: GB 253418831

✓ Telephone no: 01708 451 3381

✓ Date of sale is :   08/03/yyyy

✓ Invoice No: 10701

Exercise.1) Create an account for Star Library Educationists Ltd via the **wizard option**.
Exercise.2) Create the invoice for the sales **via *Special Invoicing*** using relevant details above.

Exercise.1)
1) Click **Customers** on the panel:

And the screen below will pop-up:

Then drop down on the *New/edit* icon above

BLANK PAGE

And from from the drop down list below, select the **Wizard** option

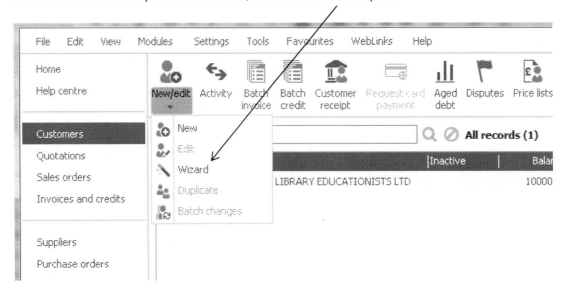

The screen below will appear;

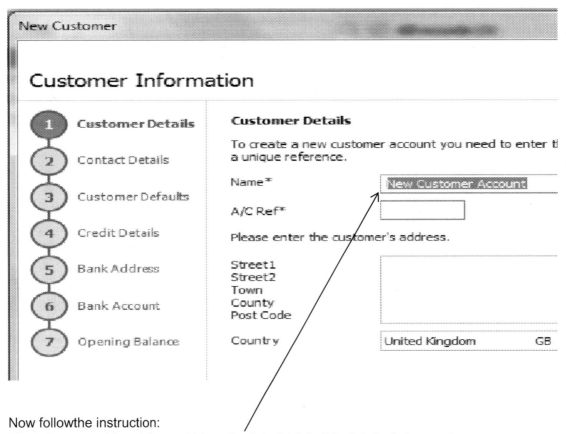

Now followthe instruction:

Enter the name (**Star Library Educationists Ltd**) in this detail window and carry on as necessary (skipping cells not necessary or compulsory as you can complete this later on). The * means compulsory and must be filled. Click **Next** and move to no 2, 3 ….At no 4, the Credit Details window, you need to check the Terms Agreed box otherwise will be alerted every time you process this customer. This can be annoying.

BLANK PAGE

Note

Exercise.2)

Click **New Invoice** in the task list and the **Product Invoice** window will appear as below:

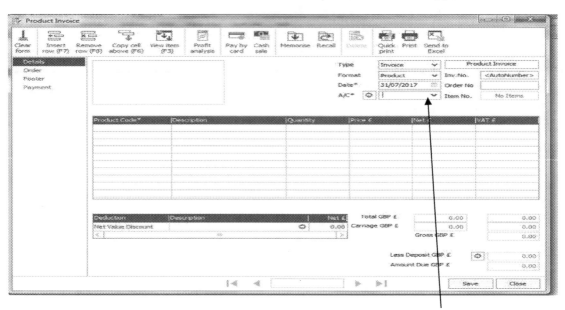

✓ Select the **Customer Account** by searching through the **Drop Down** List. As you have already created Star Library Educationists Ltd, it will appear as shown below.

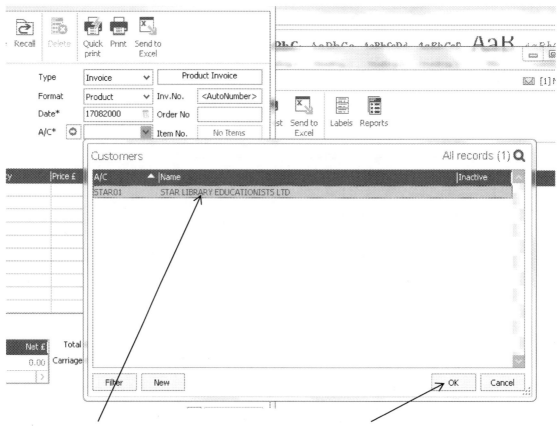

Select it by **double clicking** on it or highlight it and click the **OK** button.

BLANK PAGE

Note

The window below will appear.

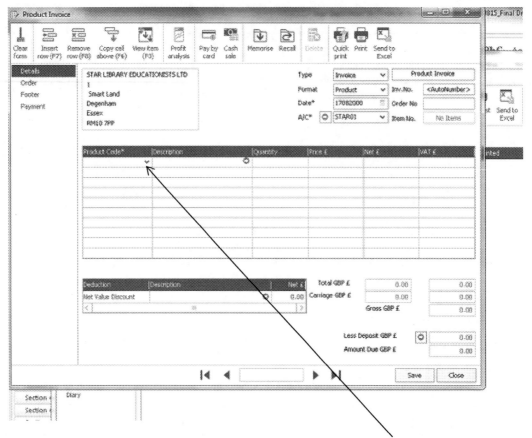

Proceed to invoice as normal using the special product line from the **drop down** list.

BLANK PAGE

This is the list from which you can choose the special product items for non-product line invoicing.

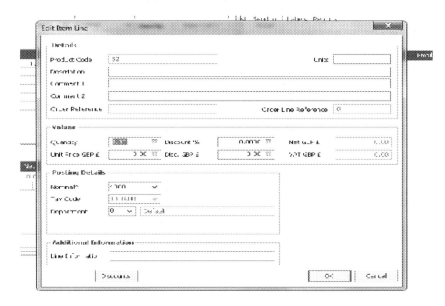

You have chosen the ***Special Product item, Tax zero rated*** because the book sale is zero rated. Click ***OK*** and continue. As can be seen from the list, **APP01** is a configured product with 200 in stock.

The screen below will appear for completion.

Complete the sales details as much as possible and click ***OK*** *(See the next screen in the next page)*

BLANK PAGE

Note

This will return you to the Product Invoice window with all the sale details as seen below:

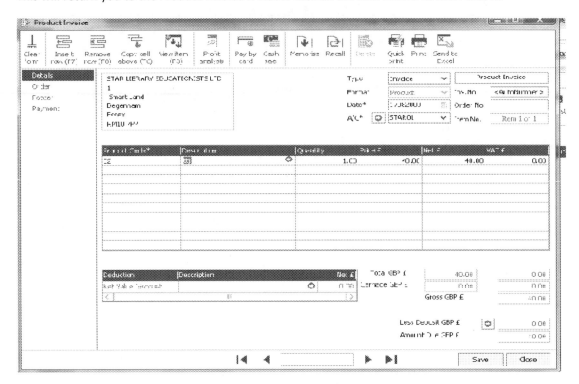

✓ Save the sales; this will print the invoice but will not update the ledger

Again use this special method of invoicing to invoice to **STAR LIBRARY EDUCATIONISTS LTD**

T- Accounts continue from page 43

T - ACCOUNTS				TRIAL BALANCE		(TB)
				T - Accounts extracted	DR	CR
9/02 -Books Sales	DR	CR				
Narration						
09/02/YYYY: UNIV01,,Sales 10 books @20 ea		200.00				
08/03/yyyy: STAR01,,400 books @ 20		8,000.00				
,						
xxx						
B/cfwd	8,200.00	-				
B/bfwd	-	8,200.00		9/02 -Books Sales	-	8,200.00
10/01 -STAR01: Star library Educationists Ltd	DR	CR				
Narration						
Books Sales:						
08/03/yyyy: 400 Book sold @ 20	8,000.00					
,						
xxx						
B/cfwd	-	8,000.00				
B/bfwd	8,000.00	-		10/01 -STAR01: Star library Educat	8,000.00	-
				Balances of accounts		
				not currently actioned here:		
-				F1/01 - Formation costs	150.00	-
				F2/01 - Director Current Account -	-	150.00
				9/01 - Bank Current A/c -1200	5,000.00	-
				0/02 - Share apital	-	5,000.00
				1/01 - Computers	1,375.00	-
				2/02 - VAT Control a/c	315.00	-
				3/01 - COMP01: Computer Land Lt	-	1,650.00
				4/01 - Stationary	200.00	-
				5/01 - OFFI01: Office Stationers Lt	-	240.00
				6/01 - BEST01: BEST PRODUCERS LT	-	15,000.00
				7/01 - Purchases	15,000.00	-
				8/01 -UNIV01: UNIVERSAL LIBRARY	200.00	-
Office use only				***Grand Total of all accounts***		
Form D				*balances to date:>>*	30,240.00	30,240.00

EXAMPLE D

Sold books to the **UNIVERSAL LIBRARY LTD** using their details to create the invoice below:

Their address: 67 Euston Road, King Cross, London NW1 9TT

VAT Reg: GB 531 288 314

Tel. No: 0207 887 2514

Transaction date: 08/04/yyyy, Our Inv. Ref: OSP10007, Sales value 1,725.00 and is

vat exempt. (**Note:** 90 books at discounted value for bulk purchase)

Invoice Universal again using the special mode of invoicing.

Click **NEW** *and the* **"create new customer window** *"will appear.*

Now continue to enter the details given line by line. (You can skip unnecessary requirement)

- ✓ Details
- ✓ Defaults (like default nominal code, Tax code e.g. T0 since book is zero rated etc.)
- ✓ Credit control (discounts, credit term e.g. 30 days etc. then click **Term Agreed)**
- ✓ Bank and then
- ✓ Memo

When you have entered as much information as necessary, click SAVE and proceed to post the invoice via **batch invoicing.**

Question

3.05   How much do UNIVERSAL LIBRARY LTD owe us?**1,950.00**

3.06   How much revenue have you generated so far from the sale of Books **9,925.00**

3.07   How much will be posted to the VAT account from the sales of 10 books? **0.00**

3.08   Is it a debit or credit figure? **Not applicable**

To ensure accurate balance of debtors, all non-batch processed invoices have to be posted.

T- Accounts continue from page 55

T - ACCOUNTS				TRIAL BALANCE		(TB)	
				T - Accounts extracted		DR	CR
8/03 -UNIV01: UNIVERSAL LIBRARY LTD	DR	CR					
Narration							
09/02/YYYY: ,,Sales 10 books @20 ea	200.00						
08/04/yyyy-,,Sold books value 1,725	1,725.00						
xxx							
B/cfwd	-	1,925.00					
B/bfwd	1,925.00	-		8/03 -UNIV01: UNIVERSAL LIBRAR		1,925.00	-
9/03 -Books Sales	DR	CR					
Narration							
09/02/YYYY: UNIV01,,Sales 10 books @20 ea		200.00					
08/03/yyyy: STAR01,,400 books @ 20		8,000.00					
08/04/yyyy: UNIV01,,Sold books value 1,725		1,725.00					
xxx							
B/cfwd	9,925.00	-					
B/bfwd	-	9,925.00		9/03 -Books Sales			9,925.00
				Balances of accounts			
				not currently actioned here:			
-							
				F1/01 - Formation costs		150.00	-
				F2/01 - Director Current Account -		-	150.00
				9/01 - Bank Current A/c -1200		5,000.00	-
				0/02 - Share apital		-	5,000.00
				1/01 - Computers		1,375.00	-
				2/02 - VAT Control a/c		315.00	-
				3/01 - COMP01: Computer Land Lt		-	1,650.00
				4/01 - Stationary		200.00	-
				5/01 - OFFI01: Office Stationers Lt		-	240.00
				6/01 - BEST01: BEST PRODUCERS LT		-	15,000.00
				7/01 - Purchases		15,000.00	-
				10/01 -STAR01: Star library Educa		8,000.00	-
Office use only				Grand Total of all accounts			
Form E				balances to date:>>		31,965.00	31,965.00

Credit notes –using the batch system

You receive a call from UNIVERSAL LIBRARY that **one book** was damaged on delivery. You agree to credit them for this book that is **priced at 20**. No. 7001 dated 05/05/yyyy.

Action

Goto Customers

Click ***Batch Credit*** on the links

From the batch Customers credit window that appears, Select UNIVERSAL LIBRARY

LTD from the Drop down List

Enter the details as given

Click **save** when finish

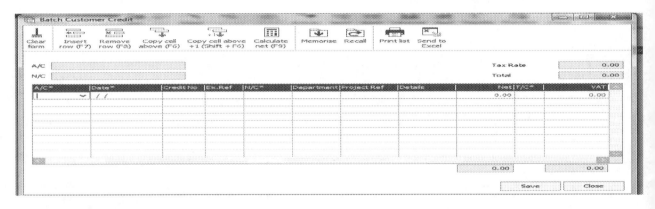

T- Accounts continue from page 57

T - ACCOUNTS			TRIAL BALANCE		(TB)
			T - Accounts extracted	DR	CR
8/04 - UNIV01: Universal Library Ltd	DR	CR			
Narration					
09/02/YYYY: ,,Sales 10 books @20 ea	200.00				
08/04/yyyy:,,Sold books value 1,725	1,725.00				
15/05/yyyy: Damaged good value 20		20.00			
xxx					
B/cfwd	-	1,905.00			
B/bfwd	1,905.00	-	8/04 - UNIV01: Universal Library Ltd	1,905.00	-
9/04 - Books Sales	DR	CR			
Narration					
09/02/YYYY: UNIV01,,Sales 10 books @20 ea		200.00			
08/03/yyyy: STAR01,,400 books @ 20		8,000.00			
08/04/yyyy: UNIV01,,Sold books value 1,725		1,725.00			
15/05/yyyy:UNIV01,, Damaged good value 20	20.00	-			
xxx					
B/cfwd	9,905.00	-			
B/bfwd	-	9,905.00	9/04 - Books Sales	-	9,905.00
			Balances of accounts		
			not currently actioned here:		
-			F1/01 - Formation costs	150.00	-
			F2/01 - Director Current Account - D.	-	150.00
			9/01 - Bank Current A/c -1200	5,000.00	-
			0/02 - Share apital	-	5,000.00
			1/01 - Computers	1,375.00	-
			2/02 - VAT Control a/c	315.00	-
			3/01 - COMP01: Computer Land Ltd	-	1,650.00
			4/01 - Stationary	200.00	-
			5/01 - OFFI01: Office Stationers Ltd	-	240.00
			6/01 - BEST01: BEST PRODUCERS LTD	-	15,000.00
			7/01 - Purchases	15,000.00	-
			10/01 -STAR01: Star library Educatic	8,000.00	-
Office use only			**Grand Total of all accounts**		
Form F			**balances to date:>>**	31,945.00	31,945.00

Tutorial

Note: You cannot print a credit note for your **Customer** from this option. Only use this option to record credit notes that you have already credited. You should use the *Invoicing* option if you want to print a credit note to send to customer.

From the Customers window, select the Customer (or Customers) that you want to create a batch credit note for.

Click *Credit*.

The **Batch Customer Credit** window appears

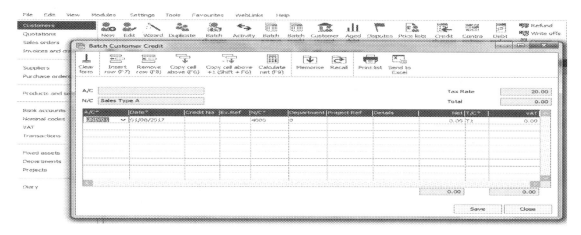

For each credit note item (or whole credit note), enter the details one line at a time. If you calculated the batch totals manually before you started entering them on to the sage line 50, check your batch total against those shown on the batch customer Credits window.

To accept the entries, click **Save.**

The details are posted to update the Nominal Ledger and the relevant customers' record.

If you do not wish to save this batch, click **Close** to clear the data and start again.

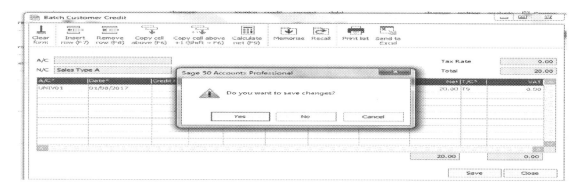

No will exit you and send you back to the customer window. Yes will save the credit. Cancel will return you to the credit window to start inputting the credit again.

The **Close** button does not cancel any batch entries you have already saved.

BLANK PAGE

Credit control process

Definition: *Credit control is the process of implementing a procedure that aimed at judging a prospect's creditworthiness in the first place so as to avoid the harder process of carrying out a procedure for extracting owed money from bad debtors*

Nevertheless, debtors have to be reminder of amount outstanding regularly to avoid balance remaining g outstanding for excessive period of time. The main action is to send statements to Customers regularly at least once a month.

To select statement for customers,

- ✓ Click ***Customers*** icon on the Menu
  - o Goto ***Documents & Reports***
  - o ***Drop down*** and select ***Statements***

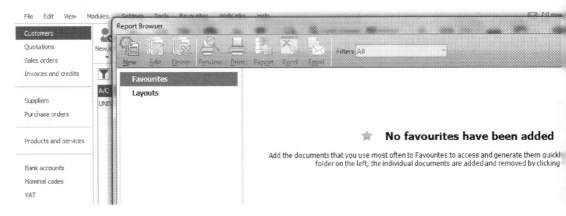

As No favourite has been selected,

Click ***Layouts***

And a host of layouts will be displayed as in the window below:

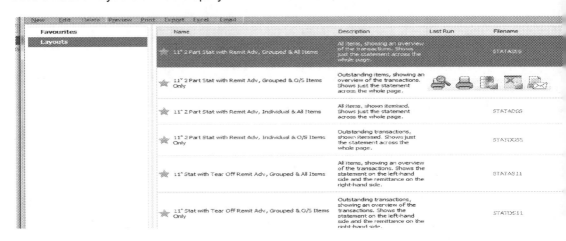

Now select the require format of your choice and continue.

BLANK PAGE

Note

Section 3.5: Invoicing for Cash Sales

Here we are referring to those sales paid for immediately (i.e. non-credit sales).

It is here recommended to first create reasonable account or accounts for cash sales. This is because Sage will not allow you to make cash sales with blank account name. Below are reasonable suggestions:
- ✓ CASH01: Cash Sales To:
- ✓ CRED01: Credit Card Sales To:
- ✓ ONLI01: On Line Sales To:

Exercise 6

When you attempt to finish sales by clicking Cash Sales after completing an invoice with a **blank account code and name**, Sage will ask you the question below.

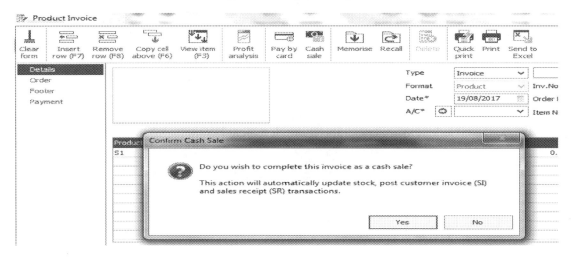

If you answer Yes and the account name is blank, the below alert will be given:

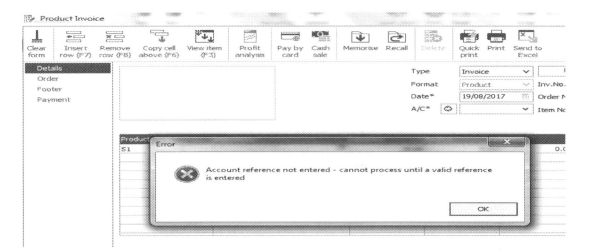

This is why the above accounts have to be set up first for non-credit sales. However if the account code and names are not blank, clicking cash sales will allow you to proceed.

BLANK PAGE

Note

Once these accounts are set up, you can now proceed to make non-credit sales as follows:

To do this, Goto **Invoice and Credits**

✓ Click **New Invoice**, and the **Product Invoice** window below will appear:

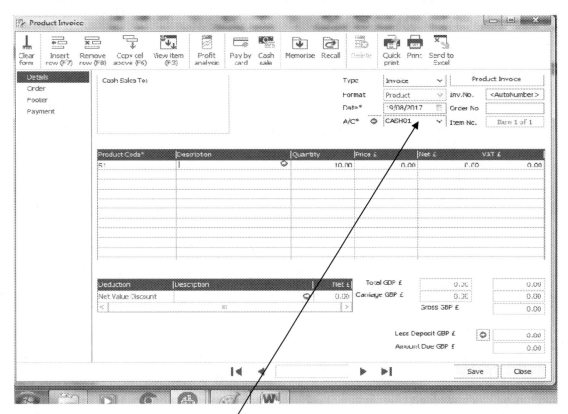

From the drop down list, select the non-credit sale account you want process.

Account code: (**Insert this code** in **A/C***)   CASH01: Cash Sales To:
Assign a **nominal code** for such sales: 4100

     (This is for analysis purposes)

BLANK PAGE

The Cash Sales Invoicing

Now proceed to make the cash sale as normal invoicing except that after creating the invoice you will choose **Cash sale** and proceed as prompted.

Creating a cash sales invoice is just like creating normal invoice.

Once you Goto *Invoice and credits*, and get to the window above, Goto the A/C* drop down box and the screen below will pop-up:

Since you have created the account, as seen above, you can now complete a cash sale. See illustration below:

✓ **Double click on** the row bearing *Cash Sales To:* account or click **OK** as arrowed above.

BLANK PAGE

Note

Proceed to invoice as normal

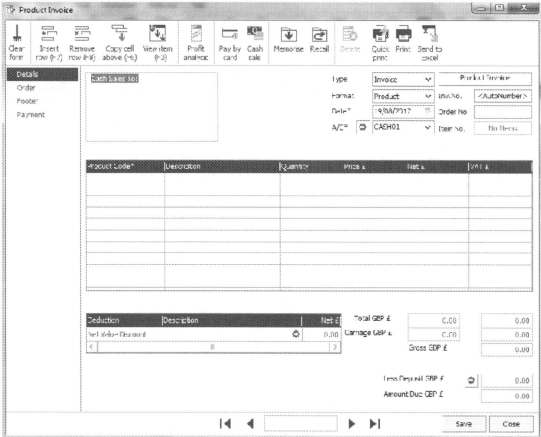

You can enter the buyer's details under the Account name (Cash Sales To :) highlighted in blue, Do not over write the account name as this will cause the invoice not to show on the invoice list.

Complete the sales details as much as possible and either:

✓ **Save** the sales; this will not update the ledger now but will save it for later action or

This can be treated as credit sales or cash sales depending on your future action.

✓ Click the **Cash sale**, this is the most likely option as this is a cash sales or

(Remember; you make non-credit sale by credit card or other means; in these cases you will Click Pay by card or the other means. In this volume you will learn the Cash sale option only.)

Once you click *Cash sale*, the followings will happen as discussed above:

BLANK PAGE

Note

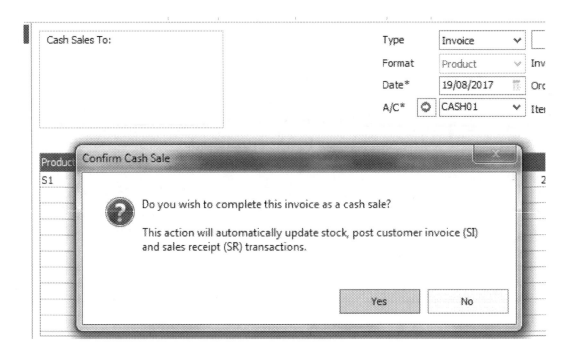

If you choose **Yes**; This will:

- ✓ apply the invoice as paid
- ✓ update the accounts
- ✓ Prompt you to print invoice immediately for the cash sales.

If you choose **No,** This will send you back (a loop)
- ✓ So you can decide if pending credit or cash sales.
- ✓ If you choose **Save,**
    - ○ This will save the sale, print details but no update

BLANK PAGE

Section 3.6: Batch Invoicing (Customers)

This is where invoices are issued outside the sage system using different means of creating invoices. Other sector of the business could have the right to invoice customers and send these invoices to the central account department for posting to the system especially where there are no direct links to the main system. It could also be a control issue.

Where this is the case, more than one invoice could be entered to various customers' accounts from one batch invoice screen.

Below are vital extracts from various so made and invoiced:

Customers Name	Account Code	Invoice date	Invoice Ref	Order Ref	Good/Ser vices	Pro Type	Nom Code	Qty	Net Amount	Vat	Gross Amount	Postal Address
David West	WEST01	21/01/2017	OSP1017/2101	David	Books	Product	4000	12	240	0	240	N/a
Gbenga Onobanjo	ONOB01	21/01/2017	OSP1017/2102	GO	Books	Product	4000	10	200	0	200	N/a
Oyeayananwannie Kanu	KANU01	21/01/2017	OSP1017/2103	Oye	Books	Product	4000	2	40	0	40	N/a
Kofi Martins	MART01	22/01/2017	OSP1017/2201	Kofi	Room 12	Services	4100	1	250	50	300	N/a
Marta West	WEST02	22/01/2017	OSP1017/2201	Marta	room16	Services	4100	1	250	50	300	N/a

You are required to enter these invoices in the central sage system

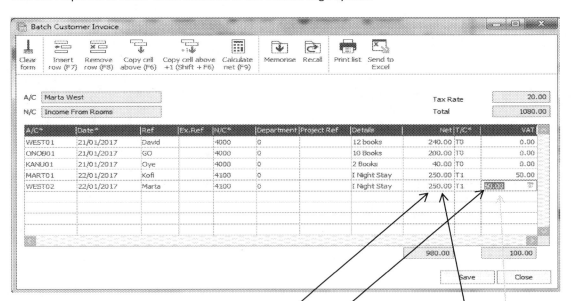

At the end of the whole batch, click **SAVE** and the entries will disappear as now posted to the various customers' account and credited to respective nominal ledger.

The double entries for each row in the batch screen can be explained using Marta West (the last entry) for explanation:

Marta West is debited with 250 net + 50 vat = 300;   300
   (She is the last consumer and bores the tax)

Nominal ledger **4100** is credited with the net income: 250

VAT (**Sales vat control account**) is credited with: 50

Please note, above entries will not appear in the T - accounts. They are for demonstration only.

T- Accounts continue from page 59

T - ACCOUNTS			TRIAL BALANCE		(TB)
			T - Accounts extracted	DR	CR
8/04 - UNIV01: Universal Library Ltd	DR	CR			
Narration					
09/02/YYYY: ,,Sales 10 books @20 ea	200.00				
08/04/yyyy:,,Sold books value 1,725	1,725.00				
15/05/yyyy: Damaged good value 20		20.00			
xxx					
B/cfwd	-	1,905.00			
B/bfwd	1,905.00	-	8/04 - UNIV01: Universal Library Ltd	1,905.00	-
9/04 - Books Sales	DR	CR			
Narration					
09/02/YYYY: UNIV01,,Sales 10 books @20 ea		200.00			
08/03/yyyy: STAR01,,400 books @ 20		8,000.00			
08/04/yyyy: UNIV01,,Sold books value 1,725		1,725.00			
15/05/yyyy:UNIV01,, Damaged good value 20	20.00	-			
xxx					
B/cfwd	9,905.00	-			
B/bfwd	-	9,905.00	9/04 - Books Sales	-	9,905.00
			Balances of accounts		
			not currently actioned here:		
	-		F1/01 - Formation costs	150.00	-
			F2/01 - Director Current Account - D.	-	150.00
			9/01 - Bank Current A/c -1200	5,000.00	-
			0/02 - Share apital	-	5,000.00
			1/01 - Computers	1,375.00	-
			2/02 - VAT Control a/c	315.00	-
			3/01 - COMP01: Computer Land Ltd	-	1,650.00
			4/01 - Stationary	200.00	-
			5/01 - OFFI01: Office Stationers Ltd	-	240.00
			6/01 - BEST01: BEST PRODUCERS LTD	-	15,000.00
			7/01 - Purchases	15,000.00	-
			10/01 -STAR01: Star library Educatic	8,000.00	-
Office use only			**Grand Total of all accounts**		
Form F			balances to date:>>	31,945.00	31,945.00

Section 4.0: Section Coverage Overview

Every business will need to operate at least one bank account. They will open current as well as saving or deposit current accounts. Current accounts are for day to day business operation whilst the others are to put excess funds away to avoid money lying idle. In addition, these non-current accounts earn interest. Though some current accounts do.

In this section, you will learn to set up bank and cash account on sage, how receipts and payments transactions are recorded and the reconciliation of cashbook balances to bank statements.

Section 4.1: Setting up bank account

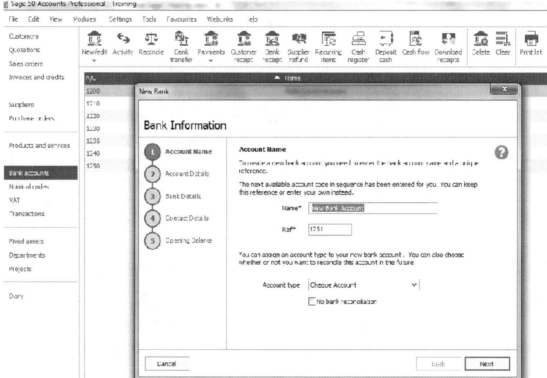

The best way is to follow the **Wizard.**

- ✓ Goto **Bank accounts**
- ✓ Drop down on the **New/Edit** icon
- ✓ Select the **Wizard** and the window above pops up.

Enter all necessary information such as:

- ✓ Bank Name
- ✓ Account number
- ✓ Opening balance etc.
- ✓ Click **Next** and continue (skipping non-compulsory details as these can be done later)
- ✓ When you finish, Click **Save.**

BLANK PAGE

Section 4.2: Bank Receipts and payments in form of cheque, Cash, Credit cards etc.

In this Section, you will learn to record transactions in the bank and cash accounts.

When accepting money from payers or making payments to others, it is vital to specify which account to used.

Click **Bank Accounts**

From the above,

Highlight Bank Current Account – 1200 (if this is the account to use)

If you are happy with the bank highlighted, then proceed to perform the operation.

At the window above, you can access individual bank account by simply double clicking on the line or click the **OK** button to proceed.

You can perform different operations by clicking on any of these icons. For example, if you drop down on New/**Edit** icon below, you can:

Create a new account, 2) Edit an existing account, 3) use the wizard or 4) duplicate.

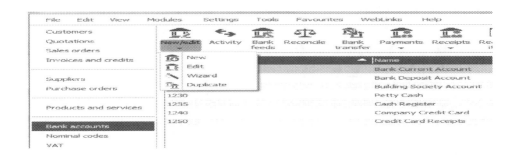

BLANK PAGE

Note

Assuming an opening balance of 5,000 from D.D Onward for the purchase of shares has not been entered in the Cashbook, from the beginning, you can add this by:

Clicking on the **Edit** icon

Goto "**OB**"

Post the relevant entries

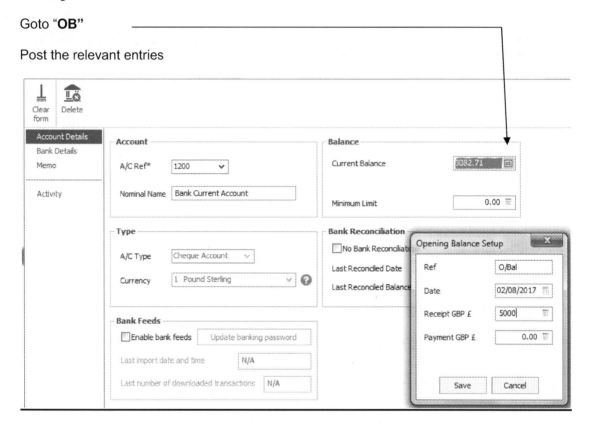

Now Click **Save** and the account will be up dated.

BLANK PAGE

Section 4.3: Paying our Suppliers
(This action will reduce our Creditors / Payable balance in the balance sheet)

Tutorial / Summary

Select **Bank accounts** from the Menu List.

Exercise 2

You want to pay COMPUTER LAND 1,000

You are going to use cheque no. 00001

Today's date is 10/06/yyyy.

Practical / Summary

Goto **Bank**

✓ Select / Highlight the bank you want to use – **Bank Current Account**

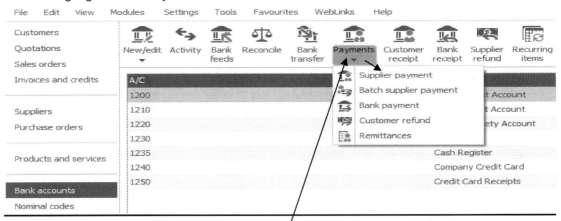

As shown above, Goto **Payment** Icon and from the Drop down

✓ Select **supplier payment** and the screen below will appear:

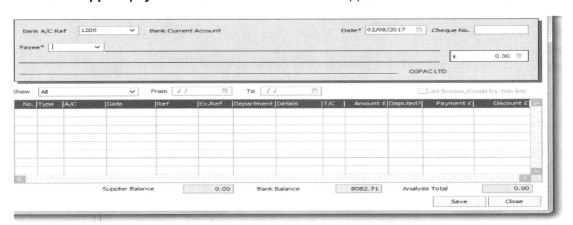

BLANK PAGE

Now select the supplier from the **Payee** as shown below

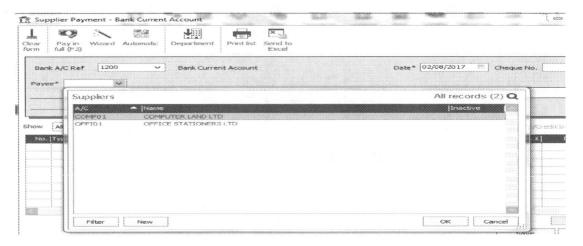

✓ Select **COMPUTER LAND LTD**

Invoices from COMPUTER LAND LTD will appear as shown below.

There is only one invoice so far from Computer Land Ltd for 1,650.00.

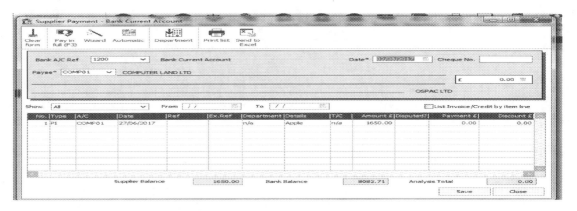

     ✓ Enter the date for this payment
     ✓ Enter the cheque number in the cheque number box
     ✓ Enter 1000 in the amount box
     ✓ Enter 1000 in the **Payment box** on the row of the item to pay
     ✓ Then click **Save.**

You have now successfully paid COMPUTER LAND LTD 1,000.00. The outstanding balance should be 650.00.

BLANK PAGE

Note: If you don't perform the above line "Enter 1000 in the **Payment box** on the row of the item to pay", and Click **Save,** the below screen will popup:

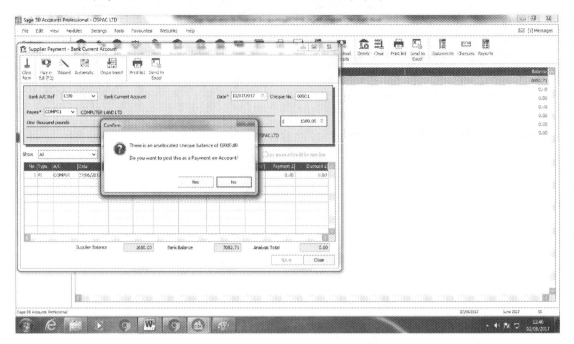

BLANK PAGE

If you answer *Yes*, the amount will not be allocated to any invoice. Allocation will have to be done at a later stage.

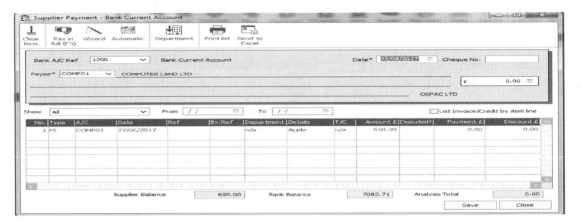

The screen below displays the activity of COMPUTER LAND LTD so far:

The items above the **divide** show all business transactions with COMPUTER LAND LTD. You will notice an item in red. This is a deleted posting and will not be considered in any calculation. So ignore this. (Sage keeps record of ALL postings so only post when you are sure)

The items below the divide show each payment and how they have been applied to truncations above the divide.

BLANK PAGE

Note

Remittance advice

When you use the **wizard**, it will open up the screen below:

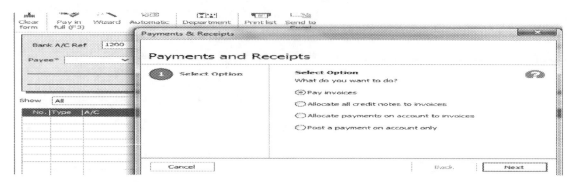

From here, you can choose the option you want. Click next and complete the details required. Receipt/remittance can be attached to paymemnts.

Exercise 3

On the 10/07/yyyy, another cheque no, 00002 was issued for 150.00 to COMPUTER LAND LTD. Another payment for 100.00 was made to same supplier; cheque no. 000003 dated 15/07/yyyy.

Task

Post these payments to sage account.

Question

4.01   What is the balance on COMPUTER LAND LTD account now? **400**

T- Accounts continue from page 75

T - ACCOUNTS			TRIAL BALANCE	(TB)	
			T - Accounts extracted	DR	CR
11/01 - Bank Current A/c -1200	DR	CR			
Narration					
Opening Balance	5,000.00				
10/06/yyyy: COMP01,,,cq00001	-	1,000.00			
10/07/yyyy: COMP01,,,cq00002		150.00			
15/06/yyyy: COMP01,,,cq00003		100.00			
xxx					
B/cfwd	-	3,750.00			
B/bfwd	3,750.00	-	11/01 - Bank Current A/c	3,750.00	-
3/02 - COMP01: Computer Land Ltd	DR	CR			
Narration					
3 Laptops @ 550 ea incl-vat		1,650.00			
10/06/yyyy:,,,cq00001	1,000.00				
10/07/yyyy:,,,cq00002	150.00				
15/06/yyyy: ,,,cq00003	100.00				
xxx					
B/cfwd	400.00	-			
B/bfwd	-	400.00	3/02 - COMP01: Computer l	-	400.00
			Balances of accounts		
			not currently actioned here:		
	-				
			F1/01 - Formation costs	150.00	-
			F2/01 - Director Current Acc	-	150.00
			9/01 - Bank Current A/c -1200		-
			0/02 - Share apital	-	5,000.00
			1/01 - Computers	1,375.00	-
			2/02 - VAT Control a/c	315.00	-
			4/01 - Stationary	200.00	-
			5/01 - OFFI01: Office Station	-	240.00
			6/01 - BEST01: BEST PRODUC	-	15,000.00
			9/04 - Books Sales	-	9,905.00
			8/04 - UNIV01: Universal Lib	1,905.00	-
			7/01 - Purchases	15,000.00	-
			10/01 -STAR01: Star library	8,000.00	-
Office use only			*Grand Total of all accounts*		
Form G			*balances to date:>>*	30,695.00	30,695.00

From the Bank Account window, select the bank account you wish to use to pay your supplier, and then click **supplier payment**.

The **supplier Payment** window appears:

This also displays the name of the selected bank account.

Enter the payments details.

Allocate the money paid to the individual invoices items displayed in the table by entering a value in the Payment box of each. You can Part pay an invoice item or pay it in full, but you cannot allocate more than the full value of the item. If you are paying an item in full, click on the item payment box then click pay in Full. The amount needed to pay the item in Full is the entered for you automatically.

Continue allocating money in this way until all the money you entered in the cheque amount box is used up.

If you have been given discount against an invoice item, enter the discount amount (not the percentage figure) in the discount box. For example, this may have been offered to you for early payment. The analysis will decrease by the amount of any discount value entered. This may mean that you can allocate more of the amount you entered in the cheque amount box against further invoice items (but from the same supplier).

If you have not selected "Always Create Remittance" within your Bank Defaults, and you want to print a remittance advice note, Click Create Remittance. This saves the remittance information. To print your remittance advice note, follow the instructions given in the section To Print a Supplier

Remittance Advice Note.

When making payments, you can use the *Wizard option* to make payment and generate receipts.

Choose the way you want to pay from the list and choice *Next*

The fill in the details required and the *Pay.*

BLANK PAGE

Section 4.4: Receiving from our Customers

(This action will reduce our debtors / Receivable balance in the balance sheet)

You have just received payment for the sale to STAR LIBRARY EDUCATIONISTS LTD for 5,000.00 and need to record this in our books. Receipt dated 28/07/yyyy.

Action

Goto Bank

- ✓ Select / highlight the Bank you need to use – **Bank Current Account**
- ✓ From the **Receipts** drop down list,
- ✓ Select **Customers Receipts** and the Customers *Receipt* window will pop-up:

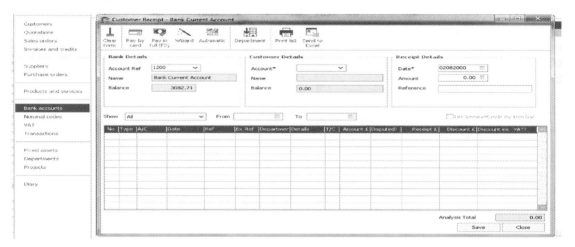

From the **Account*** A/C Drop down list, select Star Library Educationists Ltd

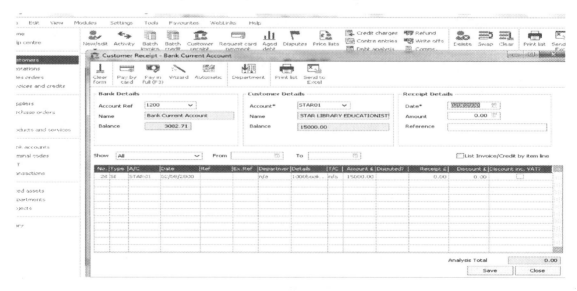

The invoice for 15,000.00 appears (This appears to be the only invoice from the customer otherwise ALL invoices from it will surface for attention.

BLANK PAGE

Note

Enter the date you received the payment – **28/07/yyyy.**

Enter the cheque/ remittance ref: in the cheque number box

Enter **5,000.00** in the **Amount** box

- ✓ Click on the **Receipt** box of the item for which payment is received.
- ✓ Click **Automatic,** Then click **Save.**

You have now successfully recorded receipt from STAR LIBRARY EDUCATIONISTS LTD for 5,000. The outstanding balance should be **3,000.**

T Accounts continues from page 91

T - ACCOUNTS				TRIAL BALANCE	(TB)	
				T - Accounts extracted	DR	CR
11/02 - Bank Current A/c -1200	DR	CR				
Narration						
Opening Balance	5,000.00					
10/06/yyyy: COMP01,,,cq00001	-	1,000.00				
10/07/yyyy: COMP01,,,cq00002		150.00				
15/06/yyyy: COMP01,,,cq00003		100.00				
28/07/yyyy: STAR01,,,receipt 5,000	5,000.00					
xxx						
B/cfwd	-	8,750.00				
B/bfwd	8,750.00	-		11/02 - Bank Current A/c -1200	8,750.00	-
10/02 -STAR01: Star library Educationist	DR	CR				
Narration						
Books Sales:						
08/03/yyyy: 1,000 Book sold @ 20	8,000.00					
28/07/yyyy:,,,receipt 5,000		5,000.00				
xxx						
B/cfwd	-	3,000.00				
B/bfwd	3,000.00	-		10/02 -STAR01: Star library Educatio	3,000.00	-
				Balances of accounts		
				not currently actioned here:		
	-			F1/01 - Formation costs	150.00	-
				F2/01 - Director Current Account - D.	-	150.00
				0/02 - Share apital	-	5,000.00
				1/01 - Computers	1,375.00	-
				2/02 - VAT Control a/c	315.00	-
				4/01 - Stationary	200.00	-
				5/01 - OFFi01: Office Stationers Ltd	-	240.00
				9/04 - Books Sales	-	9,905.00
				8/04 - UNIV01: Universal Library Ltd	1,905.00	-
				3/02 - COMP01: Computer Land Ltd	-	400.00
				6/01 - BEST01: BEST PRODUCERS LTD	-	15,000.00
				7/01 - Purchases	15,000.00	-
Office use only				***Grand Total of all accounts***		
Form H				***balances to date:>>***	30,695.00	30,695.00

Section 4.5: Other Bank Payments / Receipts

(Adhoc money exchanges from business associates not carried as such in our books neither as creditors nor debtors)

<u>Financial accounting reaction to such occurrences</u>

These will be such things like:

<u>Payments</u>

- ✓ insurance payments which passes thru as direct debits (DD)
  - o **Journal Action:** Debit Insurance; Income statement item; Cr Bank; balance sheet item
- ✓ Rent payments for which you could set up a standing order for (SO)
  - o **Journal Action:** Debit Rent; Income statement item; Cr Bank; balance sheet item
- ✓ Telephone payments mostly by DD
  - o **Journal Action:** Debit Telephone; Income statement item; Cr Bank; balance sheet item
- ✓ Bank charges for services rendered
  - o **Journal Action:** Debit Bank charges; Income statement item; Cr Bank; balance sheet item

<u>Receipts</u>

- ✓ Donations received from concerned donors
  - o **Journal Action:** Debit Bank; balance sheet item , Credit Donations; Income Statement item
- ✓ Investment income such as dividend etc.
  - o **Journal Action:** Debit Bank:; balance sheet item , Credit Investment income; Income Statement item
- ✓ VAT refunds from HMRC
  - o **Journal Action:** Debit Bank:; balance sheet item , Credit VAT liability; Also Balance Sheet item
- ✓ Bank Interest received
  - o **Journal Action:** Debit Bank:; balance sheet item , Credit Interest received; Income Statement item

BLANK PAGE

Sage treatments of such transactions

(To mirror above accounting double entries adjustments)

Bank Payments
Use the **Bank payment** option to record all bank payments you make that do not involve a supplier account e.g. payments you have made from your bank, cash credit card accounts for petrol, donations and so on.
All you need to keep track of where your money goes, is to select the bank, cash or credit card account you want to pay from and enter the payments in the transaction entry window that appear. Sage line 50 takes care of the accounting procedures for you just as you did above in the financial accounting reaction double entry system.

Each payment can be made up of many individual transactions, each one posted to a different nominal account if required. This feature is very useful, if you want to analyse where your money is going.

BLANK PAGE

Note

Exercise 4

I.   The sale manager gave you a parking ticket he was issued went for a meeting in the City. The ticket was 100 and dated 26/06/yyyy with reference no. PAYB4UPAC. If he pays within 14 days a reduced penalty of 50 will be acceptable by the issuing authority. Nominal code 7304 is in use for such items. Assume the date is 6 day after the issue and you can take advantage of the 50% discount for early settlement using cheque no. 00004

Assume the date is 6 day after the issue and you can take advantage of the 50% discount for early settlement using cheque no. 00004

II.   Three cheques dated 29/07/yyyyhave also been issued for salary to the following staff:

    a. No. 00005 for 2,550.00 to Jones Gilbert
    b. No. 00006for 2,050.00 to Tom Wilson
    c. No. 00007for   950.00 to Jacky Smiths

Required

Post these transactions using the bank option. (Use – Bank Current Account)

Action

Click the required *bank Payment*

Select the appropriate bank account

Enter the nominal code for the payments and post according

T- Accounts continue from page 97

T - ACCOUNTS			TRIAL BALANCE	(TB)	
			T - Accounts extracted	DR	CR
11/03 - Bank Current A/c -1200	DR	CR			
Narration					
Opening Balance	5,000.00				
10/06/yyyy: COMP01,,,cq00001	-	1,000.00			
10/07/yyyy: COMP01,,,cq00002		150.00			
15/06/yyyy: COMP01,,,cq00003		100.00			
28/07/yyyy: STAR01,,,receipt 5,000	5,000.00				
10/06/yyyy: 7304,,, Ticket Council,cq00004		50.00			
29/07/yyyy:,,,cq0004-to Jones Gilbert		2,550.00			
29/07/yyyy:,,,cq0005-to Tom Wilson		2,050.00			
29/07/yyyy:,,,cq0004-to Jacky Smiths		950.00			
xxx					
B/cfwd	-	3,150.00			
B/bfwd	3,150.00	-	**11/03 - Bank Current A/c -1200**	3,150.00	-
13/01 - 7304: Motor Expense	DR	CR			
Narration					
10/06/yyyy:,,, Ticket Council,cq00004	50.00				
xxx					
B/cfwd	-	50.00			
	50.00	50.00			
B/bfwd	50.00	-	**13/01 - 7304: Motor Expense**	50.00	-
14/01 - Wages & salaries	DR	CR			
Narration					
29/07/yyyy:,,,cq0004-to Jones Gilbert	2,550.00				
29/07/yyyy:,,,cq0005-to Tom Wilson	2,050.00				
29/07/yyyy:,,,cq0004-to Jacky Smiths	950.00				
xxx					
B/cfwd	-	5,550.00			
	5,550.00	5,550.00			
B/bfwd	5,550.00	-	**14/01 - Wages & salaries**	5,550.00	-
			Balances of accounts		
			not currently actioned here:		
-					
			F1/01 - Formation costs	150.00	-
			F2/01 - Director Current Account - D	-	150.00
			0/02 - Share apital	-	5,000.00
			1/01 - Computers	1,375.00	-
			2/02 - VAT Control a/c	315.00	-
			4/01 - Stationary	200.00	-
			5/01 - OFFi01: Office Stationers Ltd	-	240.00
			9/04 - Books Sales	-	9,905.00
			8/04 - UNIV01: Universal Library Ltd	1,905.00	-
			3/02 - COMP01: Computer Land Ltd	-	400.00
			10/02 -STAR01: Star library Educati	3,000.00	-
			6/01 - BEST01: BEST PRODUCERS LTD	-	15,000.00
			7/01 - Purchases	15,000.00	-
Office use only			*Grand Total of all accounts*		
Form I			*balances to date:>>*	30,695.00	30,695.00

Bank Receipts

Receipts for:-

> Things you have not invoiced
> Interest or dividends received
>
> Insurance claims
>
> Grants.

EXAMPLE E

The Transport manager gave you an envelope and said guess what is inside? You opened it and discovered the GREAT INSURANCE CO. has settled the company 5,500.00 for damage to the company bus. But before you send it to the bank, make the necessary entries in the sage account for the receipt. The cheque is dated 25/07/yyyy with a reference no. REWC0888. Nominal code 4903 is in use for such items.

Required

Post this transaction using the Bank Receipts option. (Use – Bank Current Account)

Question

4.06   What is your bank balance now?**8,650**

Tutorial

Use the New Receipt option in the Bank navigation group to record any money you receive that is not to pay invoices you have sent, e.g. interest or dividends received or money received for an insurance claim you made, or for a grant.

You can record details of this money into one or more of the different nominal account. By allocating your income to different accounts you can see at a glance the different source of your money, how much you are receiving from each source, and when.

T- Accounts continue from page 103

T - ACCOUNTS			EXTENDED TRIAL BALANCE	(TB)	
			T - Accounts extracted	DR	CR
11/03 - Bank Current A/c -1200	DR	CR			
Narration					
Opening Balance	5,000.00				
10/06/yyyy: COMP01,,,cq00001	-	1,000.00			
10/07/yyyy: COMP01,,,cq00002		150.00			
15/06/yyyy: COMP01,,,cq00003		100.00			
28/07/yyyy: STAR01,,,receipt 5,000	5,000.00				
10/06/yyyy: 7304,,, Ticket Council,cq00004		50.00			
29/07/yyyy:,,,cq0004-to Jones Gilbert		2,550.00			
29/07/yyyy:,,,cq0005-to Tom Wilson		2,050.00			
29/07/yyyy:,,,cq0004-to Jacky Smiths		950.00			
25/07/yyyy:,,,,Great Ins Co-rewco88, Damage	5,500.00				
xxx					
B/cfwd	-	8,650.00			
B/bfwd	8,650.00	-	11/03 - Bank Current A/c -1200	8,650.00	-
15/01 - Miscellaneous Income	DR	CR			
Narration					
25/07/yyyy:,,,Great Ins Co-rewco88, Damages		5,500.00			
xxx					
B/cfwd	5,500.00	-			
	5,500.00	5,500.00			
B/bfwd	-	5,500.00	15/01 - Miscellaneous Income	-	5,500.00
			Balances of accounts		
			not currently actioned here:		
-					
			F1/01 - Formation costs	150.00	-
			F2/01 - Director Current Account - [	-	150.00
			0/02 - Share apital	-	5,000.00
			1/01 - Computers	1,375.00	-
			2/02 - VAT Control a/c	315.00	-
			4/01 - Stationary	200.00	-
			5/01 - OFFI01: Office Stationers Ltd	-	240.00
			9/04 - Books Sales	-	9,905.00
			8/04 - UNIV01: Universal Library Ltd	1,905.00	-
			3/02 - COMP01: Computer Land Ltd	-	400.00
			10/02 -STAR01: Star library Educati	3,000.00	-
			6/01 - BEST01: BEST PRODUCERS LTD	-	15,000.00
			7/01 - Purchases	15,000.00	-
			14/01 - Wages & salaries	5,550.00	-
			13/01 - 7304: Motor Expense	50.00	-
Office use only			**Grand Total of all accounts**		
Form J			*balances to date:>>*	36,195.00	36,195.00

Section 4.6: Bank Reconciliation

Bank reconciliation is the process of checking that all items paid and received have cleared through the bank and that items appearing in the bank not yet taken account of by the business are treated judiciously. Differences between the cash book and the bank statement arise: (BPP Learning Media, 2016) for three reasons:

- ✓ Errors – usually in the cash book
- ✓ Omissions – such as bank charges not posted in the cash book
- ✓ Timing differences – such as un-presented

Above is an important management tool as it highlights most importantly, payments that are yet to be accounted for in the cash book. By knowing this, the danger of getting to an unauthorised overdraft situation can be avoided. It is therefore very important that reconciliation is carried out periodically.

Unmatched items are called un-reconciled items
- o Un-reconciled payments are payments you made that are yet to be taken from our bank account. (Called payments in transits)
- o Un-reconciled receipts are receipts you have paid into our bank account but are yet to be shown as credited .(Called receipts in transits)

To perform the reconciliation on sage,

Goto **Bank accounts**
- ➤ Highlight the bank you want to reconcile
- ➤ Click **Reconcile**

And the window below will pop-up:

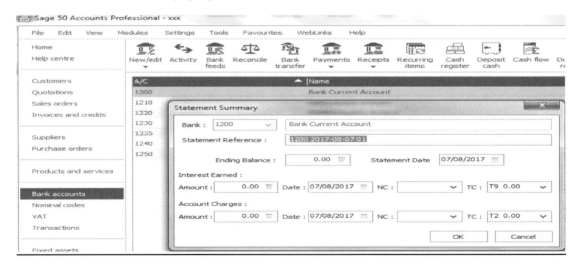

- ➤ Complete the cells and

Click **OK,**

Now you can continue to match items in the cash book to those in the bank statements.

BLANK PAGE

Note

Bank reconciliation example

Below is a bank statement to date

OSPAC LTD Bank statement for the period to 29/07/yyyy					
Date		Dr.	Cr.	Balance £	Dr/Cr
					Cr=In Money
01/06/yyyy	B/bfwd		5,000.00	5,000.00	Cr
10/06/yyyy	cq00001	1,000.00		4,000.00	Cr
17/06/yyyy	cq00003	100.00		3,900.00	Cr
18/07/yyyy	cq00002	150.00		3,750.00	Cr
01/07/yyyy	cq00004	50.00		3,700.00	Cr
29/07/yyyy	cq00007	950.00		2,750.00	Cr
28/07/yyyy	rewco88-Great Insu		5,500.00	8,250.00	Cr
28/07/yyyy	Interest		16.79	8,266.79	Cr
28/07/yyyy	DD - BT	215.05		8,051.74	Cr
29/07/yyyy	Online payment-STAR LIB	5,000.00		13,051.74	Cr

Items highlighted in light grey are matched to the Cash Book. Those in dark grey are not matched.

Below is our up to date Cash book (That is our recorded general ledger bank account)

T - ACCOUNTS		
11/04 – Bank Current A/c -1200	DR	CR
Narration		
Opening Balance	5,000.00	
10/06/yyyy: COMP01,,,cq00001	–	1,000.00
10/07/yyyy: COMP01,,,cq00002		150.00
15/06/yyyy: COMP01,,,cq00003		100.00
28/07/yyyy: STAR01,,,receipt,,sto1 5,000	5,000.00	
10/06/yyyy: 7304,,, Ticket Council,cq00004		50.00
29/07/yyyy:,,,cq0005-to Jones Gilbert		2,550.00
29/07/yyyy:,,,cq0006-to Tom Wilson		2,050.00
29/07/yyyy:,,,cq0007-to Jacky Smiths		950.00
25/07/yyyy:,,,Great Ins Co-rewco88, Damages	5,500.00	
xxx		
B/cfwd	–	8,650.00
	15,500.00	15,500.00
	8,650.00	–

Items highlighted in light grey are matched to the bank statement. Those in dark grey are not matched.

Bank Reconciliation		
Opening Cash Book Balance = B/Bfwd		5,000.00
Add: Receipts		10,500.00
		15,500.00
Deduct: Payments		(6,850.00)
		8,650.00
Add: Unmatch receipts from bank statement		
Interest		16.79
Online payment-STAR LIB		5,000.00
		13,666.79
Deduct: Unmatched payments from bank statement		
DD - BT		(215.05)
		13,451.74
Closing Bank Statement Balance=B/Cfwd		13,051.74
Add: Unmatch receipts from Cash Book		
28/07/yyyy: STAR01,,,receipt,,sto1 5,000		5,000.00
		18,051.74
Deduct: Unmatched payments from CashBook		
29/07/yyyy:,,,cq0005-to Jones Gilbert	2,550.00	
29/07/yyyy:,,,cq0007-to Jacky Smiths	2,050.00	(4,600.00)
		13,451.74

Reconcile the sage bank current account above to the bank statement. Match items from the sage A/c to the bank statements:

- ✓ Sage Bank account against Bank Statement for those items that match
- ✓ Sage Bank account items that DO NOT match to bank statements

NOW post any item not ticked in the bank statement to that sage bank account as usual. (**Note** this could be done via the reconciliation window. However it is better to do this outside the window so ALL un-ticked items can be posted comprehensively)

Establish the difference between the sage bank account and the bank statements.

Categorise the difference by performing the exercise below:

Exercise 5

List the un-reconciled receipts:

Date	Reference/Description:	Amount
28/07/yyyy	STAR01,,,receipt,,sto1 5,000	5,000

List the un-reconciled payments:

Date	Reference/Description:	Amount
29/07/yyyy	29/07/yyyy:,,,cq0005-to Jones Gilbert	2,550.00
29/07/yyyy	29/07/yyyy:,,,cq0007-to Jacky Smiths	2,050.00

BLANK PAGE

Note

<u>Tutorial</u>

The process of matching your computer bank records with those shown on your bank statement is commonly called Bank Reconciliation.

Bank Reconciliation lets you see any of your payments and receipts that have not been processed by your bank, and so acts as a check of the transactions you have entered.

As you check through, you can also add any transactions you have forgotten, or those, which the bank has added such as bank charges and interest payments, directly into Sage line 50. You can also adjust any errors you may have made.

BLANK PAGE

Note

Section 5.0: Section Coverage Overview

> *To ensure compliance with the accrual principle of presentation of financial statements, you will look into the procedure for checking that income and expenses are considered in the period they took place. Accruals and prepayments adjustments will be considered in this vein. Month End routines will be explained. It involves tiding up for management report and to ensure errors are correctly early in the period to avoid spending unnecessary time to detect before trails are lost or compromised.*
>
> *Assets are vital base of operations and need to be properly managed. You will learn how to add, depreciate and remove assets. Where Sage is in operation, full details of assets have to be recorded to make them active for proper running of the double entries system of accounting.*
>
> *The bank will also be visited here it terms of reconciliation. You will learn how to manage the bank by matching items in bank statements to those from the originating cashbooks. Those alien to the cash books are scrutinised before updating to the books whilst those from the cashbook not seen in the bank statements are listed as un-reconciled receipts and payments in the current period for scrutiny in the next period.*

Section 5.1: Month End Routines

Section_3.1: Month End Procedures; Theoretically and Practically

   This will cover: Accruals Accounting
             Fixed Assets
             Nominal ledger
(Financial Accounting point of view)

Accounts are required to be prepared under the **accrual basis** so that incomes and expenses are recognised in the accounting period to which they occurred rather than on the cash basis of receipts and payments.

This basis of accounting gives rise to the following types of accounting transactions:
 I. Accrued income
 II. Accrued expense
 III. Prepaid income
 IV. Prepaid expense:

BLANK PAGE

Note

Section 5.2: Accruals and Prepayments – Financial Accounting Treatment

Explanation of Accrual and Prepayment:

Accrual is "identifying the expenses incurred in a period matched against revenues which is why this is also called the matching concept" Prepayments on the other hand happen when items other than purchases are bought for use in the business and are not fully used up in the period. (Wood & Robinson, 2009).

Below extract of an example will suffice for simple accrual and prepayment for sage entries. Please focus on the rows highlighted in yellow.

Jupiter Plc had the following trial balance at 31st July 2015

	Extracted Trial Balance		Adjustment to Trial Balance	
	DR	CR	DR	CR
Trade Payables		40,000		
Bank/Cash	12,300			
Insurance	6,000			
Provision for bad debt		2,300		
Rent	40,000			
Buildings provision for depreciation		20,000		
Motor expenses	10,000			
Salaries & wages	100,000			
Stationery	4,000			
Heat & light	7,000			
Telephone	2,000			

You are given the following additional information

a) Closing Stock is £74,000

b) Depreciation has not yet been provided

    Buildings 10% straight line

    Machinery 25% reducing balance

    Office furniture 50% straight line

c) There is an accrual for stationery of £400

d) There is an accrual of £300 for telephone expense

e) There is an accrual of £600 for interest

f) Rent for the year is £36,000 so there is a £4,000 prepayment

g) Taxation is to be £12,000 for the year

h) There is a £2,000 prepayment included in the insurance amount

Required:

a. Adjust the trial balance to take account of the above adjustments.

Solution

The double entries for the accruals and prepayments highlighted in the above question will be:

c)   **Debit** stationary with   400
        Credit Accrual – Stationary with   400
d)   **Debit** Telephone with   300
        Credit Accrual – Telephone with   300
f)   **Debit** Prepayment –Rent with   4,000
        Credit Rent with   4,000
h)   **Debit** Prepayment – Insurance with: 2,000
        Credit Insurance with: 2,000

(See the posting in the Trial balance adjustment columns below)

Jupiter Plc had the following trial balance at 31st July 2015

		Extracted Trial Balance		Adjustment to Trial Balance		Final Trial Balance	
		DR	CR	DR	CR	DR	CR
Trade Payables			40,000				
Bank/Cash		12,300					
Insurance		6,000			2000	4,000	
Provision for bad debt			2,300				
Rent		40,000			4000	36,000	
Buildings provision for depreciation			20,000				
Machinery provision for depreciation			25,000				
Office Furniture provision for depreciation			5,000				
Motor expenses		10,000					
Salaries & wages		100,000					
Stationery		4,000		400		3,600	
Heat & light		7,000					
Telephone		2,000		300		1,700	
Accrual: -	Stationry				400		
	Telephone				300		700
Prepayment: -	Rent			4,000			
	Insurance			2,000			6,000

Section 5.3: Accruals, Prepayments and clearing balances – Sage Treatment

This is taking account of unpaid express you have incurred in the period for which you have not yet been invoiced or expensed in the account. To reflect the true picture in the management account, an accrual is necessary.

Example F

At the June yyyy Month end you have received 200.00 worth of goods but as yet no purchase invoice. As you want to produce an accurate Profit & Loss and Balance Sheet Report for June, you must enter a journal to account for these goods. Use the Skeleton Journal MTCHACCRCRU.NJR to help you. To load this, from the journal entry window,

- o open the **EDIT Menu** and
- o Choose **Recall** option.
- o Choose the **MTHACCRU.NJR** journal

Enter the date as 28/07/yyyy

N/C	Description	T/C	Debit	Credit
5000	Purchases – Monthly Accrual	T9	200.00	
2100	Accruals – Monthly Accrual	T9		200.00

Jupiter Plc had the following trial balance at 31st July 2015

		Extracted Trial Balance		Adjustment to Trial Balance		Final Trial Balance	
		DR	CR	DR	CR	DR	CR
Trade Payables			40,000				
Bank/Cash		12,300					
Insurance		6,000			2000	4,000	
Provision for bad debt			2,300				
Rent		40,000			4000	36,000	
Buildings provision for depreciation			20,000				
Machinery provision for depreciation			25,000				
Office Furniture provision for depreciation			5,000				
Motor expenses		10,000					
Salaries & wages		100,000					
Stationery		4,000		400		3,600	
Heat & light		7,000					
Telephone		2,000		300		1,700	
Accrual: -	Stationry				400		
	Telephone				300		700
Prepayment: -	Rent			4,000			
	Insurance			2,000			6,000

T- Accounts continue from page 105

T - ACCOUNTS				EXTENDED TRIAL BALANCE	(TB	
				T - Accounts extracted	DR	CR
4/02 - Stationary	DR	CR				
Narration						
08/02/yyyy: OFFI01,,Stationary @	200.00					
28/07/yyyy: Stationary; accrued	400.00					
xxx						
B/cfwd	-	600.00				
	600.00	600.00				
B/bfwd	600.00	-		4/02 - Stationary	600.00	-
16/01 - Telephone	DR	CR				
Narration						
28/07/yyyy: Telephone; accrued	300.00					
xxx						
B/cfwd	-	300.00				
	300.00	300.00				
B/bfwd	300.00	-		16/01 - Telephone	300.00	-
7/02 - Purchases	DR	CR				
Narration						
09/02/YYYY:BEST01,,1,000 Books	15,000.00					
28/07/yyyy:MTHACCRU.NJR Jour	200.00					
xxx						
B/cfwd	-	15,200.00				
B/bfwd	15,200.00	-		7/02 - Purchases	15,200.00	-
17/01 - Rent	DR	CR				
Narration						
28/07/yyyy: Rent; prepaid		4,000.00				
xxx						
B/cfwd	4,000.00	-				
	4,000.00	4,000.00				
B/bfwd	-	4,000.00		17/01 - Rent	-	4,000.00
19/01 - Insurance	DR	CR				
Narration						
28/07/yyyy: Rent; prepaid		2,000.00				
xxx						
B/cfwd	2,000.00	-				
	2,000.00	2,000.00				
B/bfwd	-	2,000.00		19/01 - Insurance	-	2,000.00
15/1 - Accrual	DR	CR				
Narration						
28/07/yyyy: Stationary accrued		400.00				
28/07/yyyy: Telephone; accrued		300.00				
28/07/yyyy:MTHACCRU.NJR Journal;Purchas		200.00				
xxx						
B/cfwd	900.00	-				
	900.00	900.00				
B/bfwd	-	900.00		15/1 - Accrual	-	900.00
18/01/1 - Prepayments	DR	CR				
Narration						
28/07/yyyy: Rent; prepaid	4,000.00	-				
28/07/yyyy: Insurance; prepaid	2,000.00	-				
xxx						
B/cfwd	-	6,000.00				
	6,000.00	6,000.00				
B/bfwd	6,000.00	-		18/01/1 - Prepayments	6,000.00	-
				Balances of accounts		
				not currently actioned here:		
				F1/01 - Formation cost	150.00	-
				F2/01 - Director Curren	-	150.00
				0/02 - Share apital	-	5,000.00
				1/01 - Computers	1,375.00	-
				2/02 - VAT Control a/c	315.00	-
				5/01 - OFFI01: Office St	-	240.00
				9/04 - Books Sales	-	9,905.00
				8/04 - UNIV01: Univers	1,905.00	-
				3/02 - COMP01: Comput	-	400.00
				10/02 -STAR01: Star lib	3,000.00	-
				6/01 - BEST01: BEST PR	-	15,000.00
				14/01 - Wages & salarie	5,550.00	-
				13/01 - 7304: Motor Exp	50.00	-
				11/03 - Bank Current A/c -1	8,650.00	-
				15/01 - Miscellaneous	-	5,500.00
Office use only				*Grand Total of all accounts*		
Form K				*balances to date:>>*	43,095.00	43,095.00

Once you have rolled over into August and have received the purchase invoices previously accrued, you need to reverse the journal carried out in July otherwise the purchases will be included twice on the Profit & Loss report. Using the skeleton journal REVMTHAC.NJR, process the following:-

Enter the date as 01/08/yyyy

N/C	Description	T/C	Debit	Credit
2109	Accruals – Monthly Accrual	T9	200.00	
5000	Purchases – Monthly Accrual	T9		200.00

You are now ready to enter the original purchase invoices.

BLANK PAGE

Note

Prepayment

When payments are made in the advance which span over the month such as for rent, an adjustment is necessary to reduce the element that does not belong to the period of payment. An asset will be created in the balance to be release gradually to the profit and loss account in the period receiving the benefit.

Journals and Nominal Ledger Reversal

Nominal Ledger - Reversal
From the Nominal Ledger window, Click **Reversals.**
You are prompted to print your Nominal Ledger Day Books report and to make a backup of your data.
Note: It is recommend that you print Day Book and take a backup of your data so that you have a copy of your original data before you process the reversal.

Skeleton Journal Entry
To create skeleton journal:

- ➢ Select Company
  - ✓ New Journal
    - ❖ The nominal ledger journal Entry Window appears
    - ❖ In the boxes provided, enter the "batch" details from your journal entry

  Note: You can only save the values of your journal entry if you have selected the Copy Skeleton Journal Values check box in the defaults' Company Preference Option.

  - ✓ Click Memorise.
    - ❖ The Memorise Window appears
    - ❖ In the boxes provided, enter a filename and a description.
  - ✓ Click Save. To save your Skeleton Entry
  - ✓ Click cancel. To Exit without saving

Now you have saved your Skeleton Journal Entry, you can load this at any time.

The treatment of Sage prepayment journal is the reverse of sage accrual journal.

BLANK PAGE

Section 5.4 Clearing Turnover Figures

If this option is selected (i.e. tick)

- ✓ It will clear the turnover figures for customers, so you know the month's value

- ✓ It will clear the turnover figures for suppliers, so you know the month's value

- ✓ It will clear the figures so month's to date (MTD) will be different from the year to date (YTD)

- ✓ If you post entries pre clearing date, you will have to perform this action again

This is a procedure to indicate the value of transaction undertaken with business associates over the period. For example you may want to know at a glance how much activity you have done with a supplier over the month.

If this procedure is not performed, the month to date MTD will be equal to the year to date YTD value

Depreciation of fixed assets

This could be performed at this point if the depreciation rates and other details are set up properly in the register. Any depreciation set up is posted for the month. However this is a discussion for Level II

BLANK PAGE

Note

Section 6.0: Section Coverage Overview

This section explains the treatment of fixed assets and aims to comply with IAS 16. There are two alternative approaches provided by the standard of which the cost model is one. This stipulates that an item of fixed asset is carried at its cost minus its accumulated depreciation.

You will look at non-current assets (i.e. fixed assets), learn how they are recorded in sage and how to manually depreciate and carry them in the books

Section 6.1: Fixed Assets and Depreciations – Financial Theory

Fixed Assets

Definition: *Fixed assets are a company's tangible, non-current assets that are used in its business operations. Common example of fixed assets is plant for production.*

Apart from finding a trading location, most business will need asset for use in the business. For example, *buildings, equipment,* table, chair etc.

Depreciation

Definition: *Depreciation is the loss in value of asset due to wear and tear as a result of usage. According to IAS 16, it is "both the decline in value of an asset over time as well as the systematic allocation of the depreciable amount of an asset over its useful life,"*

This is another form of accrual. When asset are used in the business, it is vital that proportion of the asset's cost are charged to the profit and loss account each month.

Effectively, this is an "allocation of the cost of the asset to the fiscal periods that benefit from the assets' use (Albright & Ingram, 2007).

Depreciation Methods

The straight line and reducing balance method will be explained with an example below. These are the methods that will be used in sage demonstration. Others will be merely discussed.

Straight Line Method
 (% rate applied on the * **base cost** and remain fixed over the life of the asset)
Sum of Digits Method
(a block of unit value of the base cost spread at a descending sum of the digit over time)

Reducing Balance Method
(% rate applied on the NBV of the asset yielding a different but reducing figure over the time)
Declining Balance Method
(Inflated % rate applied on the NBV of the asset yielding a different but higher reducing figure compared to the reducing balance method over the time)
Note: *Base cost is the original cost of asset less salvage value at end of assets useful life if any.

BLANK PAGE

Straight Line Method

This method depreciates the value of an asset on a fixed percentage each year on the original cost. For example, if you have an asset 10,000 which is to be depreciated at the rate of 25% a year, the annual depreciation will be based on the original cost of the asset and remain the same throughout the life of the asset. The annual depreciation on a straight line method can be calculated below:

Section 6.1a: Straight Line Methods

STRAIGHT LINE METHOD

Year	Cost/NBV	Charge for period	Accummulated Depreciation Provision	Net Book Value (NBV)
o (Now)	10,000.00	–	–	10,000.00
1	10,000.00	2,500.00	2,500.00	7,500.00
2	7,500.00	2,500.00	5,000.00	5,000.00
3	5,000.00	2,500.00	7,500.00	2,500.00
4	2,500.00	2,500.00	10,000.00	–

Reducing Balance Method

Section 6.1b: Reducing Balance Method

This method depreciates the value of an asset on a fixed percentage each year. For example, if you have an asset 10,000 which is to be depreciated at the rate of 25% a year, the annual depreciation will, in the first instant, be based on the original cost of the asset. Thereafter, it will be based on the NBV (i.e. original cost less accumulated depreciation to date). The depreciation charge annually on a reducing balance method is shown below:

REDUCING BALANCE METHOD

Year	Cost/NBV	Charge for period	Accummulated Depreciation Provision	Net Book Value (NBV)
o (Now)	10,000.00	–	–	10,000.00
1	10,000.00	2,500.00	2,500.00	7,500.00
2	7,500.00	1,875.00	4,375.00	5,625.00
3	5,625.00	1,406.25	5,781.25	4,218.75
4	4,218.75	1,054.69	6,835.94	3,164.06
5	3,164.06	791.02	7,626.95	2,373.05

Theoretically the book value will never reach zero, but for all practical purposes, the write off value of an asset is reached by using a realistic percentage.

You can see from these examples that, in comparison to the straight-line method, the reducing balance method takes longer to depreciate an asset using the same annual depreciation rate. In these examples, after four years at 25% the asset has been written off by the straight-line method but has a remaining book value of 3,165 on the reducing balance method in year four.

BLANK PAGE

Note

Because Sage Line 50 calculates the depreciation every month, the annual rate of depreciation is calculated as a reducing balance 'monthly'. In the example above, the first annual depreciation amount of 2,500 will occur, but the first month will show a greater value of depreciation than the next and so on.

EXAMPLE F

Let's depreciate the computer bought earlier on. As technology changes fast, director of OSPAC LTD thinks the company will replace the computer in 5 years' time.

Using the Straight line method, record this in sage.

Question

5.01   What will be the first month depreciation? **23**

STRAIGHT LINE DEPRECIATION METHOD				
3 Computers bought at 650 ea incl of vat, so Gross =			1,650	
		vat=	275	
		net=	1,375	
Years	Cost/NBV	Depreciation Charged	Accummulated Depreciation	Net Book Value (NBV)
0	1,375		-	1,375
1	1,375	275	275	1,100
2	1,100	275	550	825
3	825	275	825	550
4	550	275	1,100	275
5	275	275	1,375	-
		1,375	1,375	
	As above is an annual calculation, The *first month depreciation* will be:			
	Year 1 charge *divided by: 12*			
	=	22.92	approximately	23.00

Note: Vat should be excluded from income and expenditure entries. It is paid and collected on behalf of the Customs and excises. Businesses will get a refund during vat return if they have paid more than they have collected. They will however account for excess vat collected over payments.

BLANK PAGE

Note

Section 6.2: Fixed Assets and Depreciations – On Sage

In this book, you will learn how to add fixed assets on sage without necessarily adding the full details that will activate the full running of the depreciation procedure. These will be done by journal only at this stage.

Section 6.3: Adding or Editing Fixed Asset Record
Asset Register

This can be initiated from **Setting, >Configuration**, then progress as directed below:

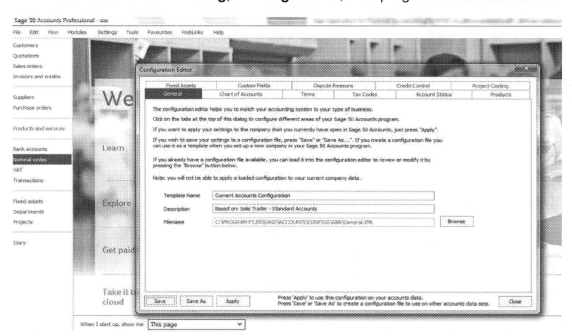

Section 6.4: Add a fixed asset record with basic details only

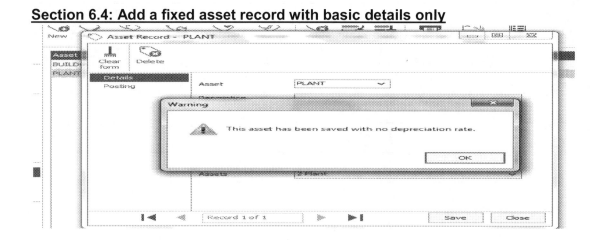

BLANK PAGE

Note

You can create a fixed asset without knowing all the depreciation details that you want to enter as alerted above by sage *and it won't become active* (you won't be able to depreciate or dispose of it) until you do enter the depreciation details.

Open: Enter New Asset.

Click into the Code field and add a unique identifying code for this asset.

Add a **description** of the asset to help your colleagues identify it. This description will be shown on reports and enquiries.

Enter the **Initial value** of the asset.

Enter the **date you purchased** the asset in the Date acquired box.

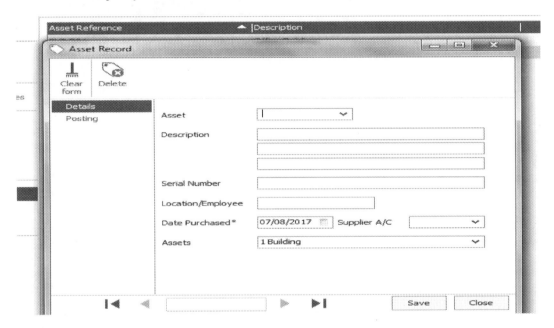

If you are entering details for an asset that has already been depreciated outside Sage 200c, enter the date it was last depreciated. Otherwise, leave this blank. When you make an asset active and post depreciation for the asset, the Last depreciated date is updated automatically.

If you want, and you have this information to hand, you can also enter the **name of the asset Manager**, the **Location** of the asset and any other information you want to record for the asset in the Analysis boxes.

Click **Save**.

BLANK PAGE

Note

Section 7.0: Section Coverage Overview

> Trial balance is the list of all the T-accounts from the general ledger of a business These are the balances of all the double entries that has passed through during the normal business transactions. In book keeping, every debit mist have a corresponding credit, As such the extraction of all the t-accounts MUST balance; hence the name Trial BALANCE.
>
> As businesses record their transactions in t-accounts (the general ledgers) there is the likelihood that errors and omissions might occur. This is first adjusted at the period end before comprehensive statements are compiled for presentation.

Section 7.1: Trial balance adjustments Exercise

It is now time to compile financial statements for OSPAC Ltd from all the transactions that went through its books up to page 105 (TB Ref: J). Being the first year of trading, there are most likely to be some accounting issues left unresolved, items erroneously misposted or inadvertently omitted. All these items need to be taken into account for the final trial balance from which comprehensive financial statements can be produced.

Let's bring forward the last TB from page 105. Here is it below:

OSPAC Ltd Trial Balance for the period to 31st December, yyyy

TRIAL BALANCE	(TB)	
T - Accounts extracted	DR	CR
11/03 - Bank Current A/c -1200	8,650.00	–
15/01 - Miscellaneous Income	–	5,500.00
Balances of accounts		
not currently actioned here:		
F1/01 - Formation costs	150.00	–
F2/01 - Director Current Account - D. D. Onward	–	150.00
0/02 - Share apital	–	5,000.00
1/01 - Computers	1,375.00	–
2/02 - VAT Control a/c	315.00	–
4/01 - Stationary	200.00	–
5/01 - OFFI01: Office Stationers Ltd	–	240.00
9/04 - Books Sales	–	9,905.00
8/04 - UNIV01: Universal Library Ltd	1,905.00	–
3/02 - COMP01: Computer Land Ltd	–	400.00
10/02 -STAR01: Star library Educationists Ltd	3,000.00	–
6/01 - BEST01: BEST PRODUCERS LTD	–	15,000.00
7/01 - Purchases	15,000.00	–
14/01 - Wages & salaries	5,550.00	–
13/01 - 7304: Motor Expense	50.00	–
Grand Total of all accounts		
balances to date:>>	36,195.00	36,195.00

The following additional information need to be adjusted for:

1.   The Miscellaneous income in the TB should be reclassified as **Insurance claims.**

2.   After meeting with his accountants, DDO has been advised that **3,500** should be charge as rent (use of home as office) to his credit.

3.   It has been realised that the furnitures used in the office were those of the director. They have been valued at **4,550**. This figure should be taken into account as introduction from the director; DDO.

4.   The reconciliation of units of books sold compared to units purchased revealed that a physical count of (1,000-10-400-90+1) 501 is in stock. This is valued at 7,515 using the first in first out inventory accounting. However it is recorded that one of them is a damaged stock returned by a customer. This has been adjusted in the sales and debtors account already but should be written off at cost of sales 15.

5.   Invoice for Light and Heat is yet to be agreed with the supplier E.ON. It is estimated that **750** should be provided for as an accrual. The following items also have to be accrued for; Telephone, Insurance, stationary at **250**, **315**, and **175** respectively

6.   Depreciation are yet to be provided: Computer at 20% Straight line method, Office Furniture at 15% reducing balance method.

7.   Nothing was prepaid.

8.   Ignore Taxation.

Required:

i.   Make the necessary adjustments to the trial balance

ii.   Prepare the statements of comprehensive income for the period to 31st December, yyyy

iii. Prepare the statement of Financial Position (Balance Sheet) as at 31st December, yyyy

The solutions

(i)

OSPAC Plc had the following trial balance at 31st December, yyyy					INCOME STATEMENT		BALANCE SHEET	
	Extracted TB		TB ADJUSTMENTS		Expenses	Income	Assets	Liabilities
	DR	CR	DR	CR	DR	CR	DR	CR
11/03 - Bank Current A/c -1200	8,650.00	-			-	-	8,650	-
15/01 - Miscellaneous Income	-	5,500.00	5,500		-	-	-	-
F1/01 - Formation costs	150.00	-			150	-	-	-
F2/01 - Director Current Account - DDO note 2	-	150.00		3,500	-	-	-	3,650
F2/01 - Director Current Account - DDO note 3	-			4,550	-	-	-	4,550
0/02 - Share apital	-	5,000.00			-	-	-	5,000
1/01 - Computers	1,375.00	-			-	-	1,375	-
2/02 - VAT Control a/c	315.00	-			-	-	315	-
4/01 - Stationary	200.00	-	175		375	-	-	-
5/01 - OFFI01: Office Stationers Ltd	-	240.00			-	-	-	240
9/04 - Books Sales	-	9,905.00			-	9,905	-	-
8/04 - UNIV01: Universal Library Ltd	1,905.00				-	-	1,905	-
3/02 - COMP01: Computer Land Ltd	-	400.00			-	-	-	400
10/02 -STAR01: Star library Educationists Ltd	3,000.00	-			-	-	3,000	-
6/01 - BEST01: BEST PRODUCERS LTD	-	15,000.00			-	-	-	15,000
7/01 - Purchases	15,000.00	-			15,000	-	-	-
14/01 - Wages & salaries	5,550.00	-			5,550	-	-	-
13/01 - 7304: Motor Expense	50.00	-			50	-	-	-
Insurance Income				5500	-	5,500	-	-
Rent			3500		3,500	-	-	-
Office furniture			4550		-	-	4,550	-
Closing stock -note 4 (BS)			7515		-	-	7,515	-
Closing stock -note 4 (COS)				7515	-	7,515	-	-
Closing stock -note 4 (COS)			15		15	-	-	-
Closing stock -note 4 (BS)				15	-	-	-	15
Light & heat - note 5			750		750	-	-	-
Telephone - note 5			250		250	-	-	-
Insurance expense - note 5			315		315	-	-	-
Accrual - Light & heat - note 5				750	-	-	-	750
Accrual - Telephone - note 5				250	-	-	-	250
Accrual - Insurance- note 5				315	-	-	-	315
Accrual - Stationary- note 5				175	-	-	-	175
Depreciation - Computer 20% SL - note 6			275		275	-	-	-
Accummulated Depn - Computer -note 6				275	-	-	-	275
Depreciation - Office Furnture 15% RB - note 6			683		683	-	-	-
Accummulated Depn - Office Furn -note 6				683	-	-	-	683
					-	-	-	-
					-	-	-	-
xxxxxxxxxxxxxx					-	-	-	-
					26,913	22,920	27,310	31,303
Profit {loss}for the period					-	3,993	3,993	-
	36,195	36,195	23,528	23,528	26,913	26,913	31,303	31,303

OSPAC LTD Income Statement for the year ended 31st December, yyyy	
Sales	9,905
Cost of sales (w1)	(7,500)
Gross Profit	2,405
Administrative expenses (w2)	(11,898)
Operating Profit / (Loss) **or** [Profit / (Loss) before interest and tax]	(9,493)
Insurance Income	5,500
Interest Expense	-
Net Profit / (Loss)	(3,993)
Taxation	-
Profit / (Loss) after tax	(3,993)

OSPAC LTD Balance Sheet as at 31st December, yyyy				
NCA		Cost	Accum Depn	NBV
Building				
Computers		1,375	(275)	1,100
Office furniture		4,550	(683)	3,867
		5,925	(958)	4,967
Current Assets				
Inventory			7,500	
Trade Receivable		4,905		
-Provision for bad debt			4,905	
-VAT Control			315	
Bank / Cash			8,650	
			21,370	
Current Liabilities				
Trade Payable		15,640		
Directors Current Account		8,200		
Accrual - Light & heat - note 5	750			
Accrual - Telephone - note 5	250			
Accrual - Insurance- note 5	315			
Accrual - Stationary- note 5	175	1,490		
			25,330	
Net current assets / (liabilities)				(3,960)
Total Asset *Less: Current liabilities*				1,007
Non-current liabilities				
Net Assets				**1,007**
Share capital & Reserve				
Share capital				5,000
Share Premium				
Retain profit (Loss):	B/fwd			
	for year		(3,993)	(3,993)
				1,007

Please note: *The notes numbers following some of the items in this exercise are for clarity only*

Workings

w1		
Cost of sales		
Opening Stock		
Purchases		15,000
		15,000
Less: Closing stock		(7,500)
		7,500
w2		
Administration Expenses		
F1/01 - Formation costs		150
14/01 - Wages & salaries		5,550
13/01 - 7304: Motor Expense		50
Rent		3,500
Light & heat - note 5		750
Telephone - note 5		250
Insurance expense - note 5		315
4/01 - Stationary		375
Depreciation - Computer 20% SL - note 6	275	
Depreciation - Office Furniture 15% RB - note 6	683	958
		11,898
SL = Straight Line		
RB = Reducing Balance		

For tax enthusiasts, some items in these financial statements are not allowed for tax. Examples are:
- × Depreciation
- × Formation costs

These items will be added back and special legislative allowances such as capital allowances deducted instead to arrive at the adjusted profit for tax.

References

Albright, T. L., & Ingram, R. W. (2007). _Financial Accounting With Journal Entries._ China: Rob Dewey.

BPP Learning Media. (2016). _FFA / ACCA Paper 3, Financial accounting._ United Kingdom: BPP Learning Media Ltd.

Picker, R., Leo, K., & Alfredson, K. e. (2013). _International Financial Reporting Standards._ India: Wiley.

Wood, F., & Robinson, S. (2009). _Bookkeeping and Accounts 7th Edition._ Harlow: FT Prentice Hall.

Printed in the United States
By Bookmasters